William Marshak

ROOKIE LOG

Cover Photo: Officers Matt Bocage, Ramin Mahboobi, Matt Snelson - 2004

ROOKIE LOG

Who They Are and Why They Do It

Follow the lives of three rookie police officers as they begin to work the streets under the guidance of Field Training Officers, veterans who will help them make the transition from student/observers to highly skilled seasoned patrol officers. The process is not easy nor success assured.

Dedication

Rookie Log is dedicated to Robert (Bob) Wasserman whose long and illustrious career in law enforcement culminated as Fremont, California Chief of Police from 1976-1992. A Korean War veteran and law enforcement officer since 1953, Wasserman rose through the ranks in several law enforcement agencies and served as president of the California Peace Officers' Association. Following retirement from law enforcement, Bob's dedication to community safety and tranquility continued when elected to Fremont City Council in 1992 and mayor in 2004. Wasserman died December 29, 2011 while serving his second term as mayor.

The short version of Bob Wasserman's legacy might read as the motto: fortitude, honesty and integrity. His life partner and wife of over 50 years, Linda remembers Bob as a guy who "never hardened" and "had a genuine respect for people." His stability, willingness to listen to others and commitment to community continue to serve as an inspiration to all who follow in his footsteps as guardians of the public.

CONTENTS

Sgt. Matt Bocage, Sgt. Ramin Mahboobi
and Lt. Matt Snelson - August 2017

Foreword

The success and effectiveness of a law enforcement agency is determined to an extraordinary extent by the character and personal depth of the people who serve as part of the organization. Lieutenant Snelson, Sergeant Mahboobi, and Sergeant Bocage, in the period that has elapsed since these articles were first published, have proven this principle through their personal commitment and dedication. The contributions they have and will make are essential components of our department and of the strength of the relationship we have with the community we serve.

During the period of time spanned by their careers, law enforcement as a profession has been called upon to confront very critical and consequential demands. Of great significance, terrorism has evolved very regrettably as a persistent threat. As another demonstration, policing has strived to develop better methods for resolving volatile situations involving subjects suffering from severe mental illness. The profession has also grown in seeking a greater understanding of the principles of implicit bias and the correlation to key issues of fundamental fairness. Of note, the progress that has occurred is in a setting of constraint with the erosion of public entity resources. Across all of what has taken place, law enforcement officers themselves have endured purposeful and focused violence of horrendous scope.

With Matt, Ramin, and Matt as representatives, our community can be proud of the way the members of our department have worked to achieve real and positive impacts for the people we serve. We can also take from their example a cognizance of the value our department places on the relationship we have with our community. Their work has included high risk operations, crisis intervention and mitigation, significant criminal investigations, use of intelligence based policing methods, applying advanced technology to public safety, facilitating peaceable assembly, working in close concert with education providers and other community entities, and helping present a spectrum of special events. As we look at what they have accomplished, we can see the way they track how policing has sought to advance across so many dimensions.

One essential aspect of most of what is achieved in law enforcement is the role of training. For our department, it has and continues to be a central aspect of our functioning and beliefs. This holds true from the perspective of the department being committed to delivering the highest levels of available training. Similarly, it reaches to individual members and leadership in terms of being dedicated to and applying training concepts. As we look at our department and California law enforcement, we can see the importance of entities such as the California Peace Officer Standards and Training and how what it provides represents an investment in our communities. It is a part of governance we absolutely must fully maintain.

At a personal level, I greatly appreciate everything Matt, Ramin, and Matt have accomplished and their influence on our department. I also really value seeing them in their role and hearing their perspective. As we look back across their careers, it is an occasion for all of us to be reminded of the dedication of the peace officers serving our respective communities and their criticality in assuring the continuity of our democracy.

Thank you for your interest in these exemplary public servants.

Richard Lucero
CHIEF OF POLICE
FREMONT POLICE DEPARTMENT

Preface

I am not sure how the idea came to me. But, the more I thought about it, the more interesting the concept became. Who are the men and women in uniform, separating and protecting most of us from the seamy side of our society? The so-called "thin blue line" of police is intriguing, frightening and essential to the establishment and maintenance of order in our lives. How are prospective police officers trained to face a daily mix of challenges from mundane to potentially lethal?

Often taken for granted and usually newsworthy in negative situations, police share an exclusive bond of camaraderie that only those who serve in the face of danger can fully appreciate and understand. Training is demanding and comprehensive for when rookies are released for solo service, they are expected to perform as veterans. Teamwork is essential, but often a single officer, first on the scene of a major incident, is expected to quickly assess and begin to control the situation while waiting for reinforcements.

When I contacted the Fremont Police Department with the idea of interviewing rookies through their field training - a steep, difficult and demanding learning curve for all new candidates - a polite "no" was a defi-nite probability. After conferring with Sergeant Clarisse Lew, I was assured

that my request would be considered by Chief Craig Steckler and shortly thereafter, was given permission to speak with three prospective Fremont Police officers following their graduation from Police Academy in Sacramento, California.

From our first introductory meeting and throughout subsequent discussions during field training and finally toward the end of their probationary period, I was able to peek into a world of tension, hard work and dedication of three extraordinary men. They gave me confidence in our police force and pride in the men and women who serve our community. I hope the following diary of thoughts by Matt Bocage, Ramin Mahboobi and Matt Snelson can give readers a sense of what it is like to put it all on the line to become a law enforcement officer. I would like to thank the Fremont Police Department and especially the three, I affectionately called "my officers" for the opportunity to listen to and record their words.

William Marshak
PUBLISHER
TRI-CITY VOICE NEWSPAPER

Introduction

I would be remiss if I didn't first take the opportunity to thank Mr. William Marshak, Publisher, of the Tri-City Voice for his on-going reporting of the hiring and training of three Fremont Police Department officers.

Officer's Ramin Mahboobi, Matt Snelson and Matt Bocage were all hired together as entry level police officers in December of 2003. The articles follow these three officers as they progress and graduate from the Sacramento Police Department Basic Academy which runs for just over twenty-seven weeks. The purpose of the basic academy is just that, to give the officers the basic skills and knowledge they will need to continue their training and education and be successful.

The officers return from the Basic Academy and are assigned to a primary Field Training Officer (FTO) as well as several other seasoned, experienced police officers who will act as their personal trainers during the eighteen week Field Training Program. We have to help the officers "unlearn" some things that they are taught in the Basic Academy and learn how we do things in Fremont. Felony traffic stops, automated report writing, criminal investigations, arrest and search warrant preparation are just some of the issues that we have to re-teach to the officers.

As you will see by the following articles, there is a strong emphasis on learning the right way to do things. The concept of teamwork which is paramount in the Fremont Police Department also comes through in the articles. You will read of the daily trials and tribulations that a new officer goes through as they mature into the job of being a Fremont Police Officer. This is a wonderful and very detailed account of the training a police officer needs to assimilate to become successful.

I would like to point out that all three officers are indicative of the high quality personnel the Fremont Police Department strives to hire as police employees for our community. These men all show through the interviews their intelligence, dedication, loyalty to Fremont citizens and sense of teamwork that all of our officers and civilian employees must have to be successful with the Fremont Police Department.

Again, my thanks to Ramin, Matt and Matt and to Mr. William Marshak for an outstanding series of articles on what it is like to become a Fremont Police Officer.

Craig T. Steckler
CHIEF OF POLICE (RET.)
FREMONT POLICE DEPARTMENT

Post Academy Interview

T hree Fremont Police Officers recently joined the department's ranks after completing a rigorous six month training course in Sacramento. TCV listened to Officers Ramin Mahboobi, Matthew Bocage and Matthew Snelson as they discussed their experiences and feelings while completing their in-house training and anticipate patrol activities. TCV will ask for comments and reactions from these officers as they move through their probationary year with the Fremont Police Department.

TCV: The standard question that comes to mind is why you decided to become a policeman.

Mahboobi: I went to school in Fremont. As a young adult, deciding on a career, I had a lot of role models from the police department - family, friends, School Resource Officer. I always wanted to work with and help people. I did a lot of research into the career and spent a few years working here as a citizen employee to get a first-hand look. The positives far outweighed any danger or negatives.

Bocage: A standard response of wanting to work with and help people while making a difference certainly applies to me. I have a background in public service - four years with the Air Force in Communications, out of high school. I just graduated from college last fall. What has played a big role was September 11th. At a time of crisis, we had a chance to see public service - fire, police, EMS - at its best. These are the type of people I want to work with. I

had an interest prior to that, but September 11th solidified my career goals and aspirations.

Snelson: I grew up in Fremont and had a good appreciation for the city and how safe it was. I majored in Psychology in college and debated whether to enter the police force or go for a Masters degree and work in family counseling. My last year in college, I started working at the church I grew up with and attend. I worked at the church full time and about a year ago, my wife and I talked about long term career goals. I did a "ride along" and decided to put in my application. Fremont and most other cities were not hiring at that time, but last October, I saw an opening on the Fremont website and applied. Fremont is one of only a few cities that I would consider for employment.

TCV: How do your families feel about your career choice?

Bocage: I have a very close relationship with my family. They and my fiancée were initially apprehensive about my decision. Everyone recognized that I had characteristics to make a good police officer, but there is always an element of danger. They adjusted very quickly and support me 100%.

Mahboobi: My family and friends have always been on the right side of the law. My family has been extremely supportive. During the process of deciding whether to pursue this career, my family said that my personality really fit and they could see me in the role. They were all supportive and encouraging.

Snelson: My family, too, has been very supportive.

TCV: Did the training program you just completed in Sacramento meet your expectations?

Bocage: With my military background, I had an idea of what to expect. It was a wonderful experience and exceeded my expectations in terms of professionalism and some of the things we heard about police academies. The academy was a fantastic training experience - tough, rigid and "hard core" - but I think we all left with a very good impression.

Mahboobi: Thankfully, Fremont took a lot of time to prepare us. Prior to going into the academy, we spent a couple of weeks in a "pre-academy." We went in prepared and knowing what to expect. I felt prepared for academy life. Right away, we were introduced to a high stress environment, received a lot of

information and were quickly tested on it, knowing that our career was on the line with each test. We spent long nights studying, memorizing and preparing for the next day including a lot of detail work preparing our uniforms for inspections.

Snelson: From the moment we walked into "pre-academy," every person we saw, bar none, would stop us and say, "If you ever need anything at the academy, call us because we have somebody who specializes in whatever you may be struggling with, whether it is physical training, arrest control baton techniques, testing materials or anything else. Every person we talked to would tell us this so I felt very supported when we were in training. We had the backing of a good department.

Mahboobi: I went in expecting a paramilitary and stressful environment. This demonstrates to yourself that you can function under stress because that is what you are going to deal with on the streets. At the same time, I was shocked and impressed by the accountability that police officers have to be under on a daily basis. Everything that you do has to be legal - you are constantly thinking about multiple things and trying to multitask. That was eye opening for me! I came out with a huge appreciation for what police are able to do. We walked out of the academy with some great training but knowing how much more I need to learn. When watching police shows, you may see the action, but not understand what is going through the officer's mind - can I search this person? Can I get in that car and search for drugs? Is this a detention, a consensual encounter or an arrest?

TCV: Not everyone completes the Police Academy. All of you were successful. What helped you complete the course successfully?

Bocage: You need a commitment to succeed. The great thing about the Fremont Police Department is they are very selective about who can become part of the organization. The camaraderie between the three of us played a huge role. There was never a doubt that we would make it. Quitting was never an option.

Mahboobi: The possibility of injury is on everyone's mind. You can be injured on week 23 and unable to pass a test, therefore out of the academy and have to start all over.

Snelson: The camaraderie is very important. Throughout the six month process, every one of us had good days and bad days. Being able to help and challenge each other made a huge difference. Out of a class of 48 candidates, the 31 who graduated had a "never quit" attitude. That is what you want in an officer because if you are in a situation where your life is at stake, you can't quit physically or mentally.

Crunch Time

After further instruction at FPD headquarters, Matthew Bocage, Ramin Mahboobi and Matthew Snelson are now on the streets of Fremont under the supervision of Field Training Officers (FTOs). With the completion of only a few days of patrol work, TCV asked for comments. Due to schedule conflicts Matthew Bocage and Ramin Mahboobi were interviewed together and Matthew Snelson at a later date.

Interview with

Matthew Bocage

Ramin Mahboobi

TCV: You've had a little bit of time on the streets. What are your impressions? Has the experience met your expectations?

Bocage: With just the little bit of exposure that I've had, it has exceeded my expectations. Last time we spoke, we hadn't been introduced to our primary FTO. Since then, we've found out who we'll be riding with and I'm happy to say that we've got some highly qualified, highly professional folks ready and eager to teach us the ropes. My primary is Officer Crandall; he's very proactive, a very busy cop with a fantastic reputation in the area. I hear he's going to keep me very, very busy. We only rode twice, and I've gotten some great exposure. We start officially on Saturday. It's going to be good. I'm a

little anxious, a little nervous. We're supposed to act as a solo officer. Initially they're going to be helping us learn the ropes, with codes and different things but the ultimate goal is for us to behave and respond like a solo officer. We're going to be pretty much doing everything.

TCV: So, right from the very beginning?

Bocage: I think it's going to depend on the primary FTO and what their teaching style is, but I know that I'm driving Saturday. I know that much. It's going to be a fast-paced learning environment for us.

TCV: Is it what you expected?

Bocage: It is. You know, there's so much going just being in the car for two days and listening to the radio traffic, dealing with everything around you, you're entire environment. It's the ultimate in multitasking. There's just so much to be paying attention to that it's a little overwhelming. From what I hear, everyone goes through that initially. It's a very steep learning curve, but I think we're ready for it. I'm cautiously optimistic.

Mahboobi: I agree with Matt. I went in there confident, yet nervous. I didn't know what to expect. I was immediately overwhelmed by it. You don't know enough to be confident yet, because it's completely different from the training we've received. It's the real thing. I've been to several calls and my FTO, Officer Koepf, looked at me and asked, "Okay, what are you going to do?" Before we even get there - we're en route - and he's already asking me how I'm going to handle the call. "Are you picturing the different types of responses you're going to be getting from the RPs (Reporting Parties) or suspects, or whoever we're going to see right now?"

I started to mentally prepare for every question he asked me about a particular call that we're about to handle. I question whether or not I have the correct answer. I just felt all of my confidence shrinking. The very first call that we were detailed, everything I thought I knew and that I would do was immediately in doubt. There was so much more to it. Nothing is simple, to sum it up. There is no routine call.

There's no simplicity at all. I immediately lost confidence and, although confident that I can do this,

when thrown to the wolves, you start to look around and wonder if you're going to get out of there. It was very overwhelming. I was doing more than I expected to have to do right off the bat. I thought I would observe a little more. The first call we had was, "It's yours, handle it!" That kind of a thing caught me off guard. Even when I thought I handled it, I took it at one degree, and there's three hundred and fifty-nine degrees that I left out. There's so much involved!

TCV: Are you critiqued after each call?

Bocage: There's a constant dialogue with our FTOs, so we're constantly in a learning/teaching environment. There's written documentation at the end of every shift that's called a Daily Observation Report. It's a check-off sheet of twenty-five or thirty items that the FTO has to go over and evaluate you on. Scale of one to seven, seven being fantastic, one being, well, you'd better start working a lot harder.

Mahboobi: There's also a "Not Responding to Training," an NRT.

Bocage: You want to totally avoid one of those.

Mahboobi: That's your zero.

TCV: Do you see this report?

Bocage: Absolutely. We're signed off on every single task that we do, every piece of documentation requires our signature. Our FTO's signature, their sergeant's signature all the way up the chain to lieutenant and captain is going to sign off on everything that we do.

TCV: Have your patrols been routine?

Bocage: Not at all, not even close. Even the simplest of tasks that we learned at the academy, that we flew through in scenario training, like just taking a simple report, when you're actually having a conversation with a real, live citizen who has concerns, it's a very different situation. They expect you to have all of the answers. I think a big part of being an officer is that the confidence level has got to be very, very high. People are counting on you to do the right thing.

TCV: What type of calls have you been on?

Mahboobi: I've had one burglary call. It was a "cold" burglary residential report. I'm in the middle of investigating that one right now to find out about a suspect. That was on my second day, and on that day my FTO said that it was my call, 100%. I'm thinking, "Wow, it's only my second day. I had more confidence on my first day." I just kind of fell back, and thought, "Okay, what have I been trained on? Go with what I know. Do what I know. Just learn from all the mistakes I'm going to make." My FTO did as he promised; he sat back and I took care of the entire call. He was there and asked questions of the Reporting Party that he felt I might have been leaving out, but for the most part, I handled everything.

After the call, we debrief everything. We talk about the plan of action on the way to the call, we handle the call, and after the call we debrief on why I did what I did, and what else I could have done. The most important thing he wants me to understand is there are several different ways to solve a problem. All can be right; you just need to know why each one is right and why others aren't. Learning, that is the challenge. That was an excellent learning call.

I've been to several "in-progress" calls and those are exciting. My very first day, I had a "245," assault with a deadly weapon. We expected resistance, but we didn't need to use any force. We took the suspect to the hospital for medical care and then to Fremont Jail for booking but, for medical reasons, we ended up at Santa Rita; I learned a lot about the booking process. Not just detaining someone, but what do you do next? An arrest on my first day within the first couple of hours!

That was like, "Well, here you go, this is what you signed up for." It didn't take long; Day One and the second call of the day. That's an example of extremes - a cold report to gather facts and the other extreme, responding "code 3" (a fight in progress), where you have to be ready to use force. That was a great eye opener. I just wanted to make sure that I did everything right. They are not breaking us in softly.

TCV: When you're in a marked car and in a uniform, do you sense a difference in how people respond to you? Are you comfortable?

Bocage: There is certainly a difference. All eyes are focused on you whether you're driving, making a stop, going into a restaurant, getting some coffee, getting some gas, wherever you may be, you're everyone's focus. You stick out like a sore thumb. That's a good thing. Police presence is what a lot of this community is looking for. It's a little awkward I suppose but it's not that big of a deal for me. It's something I got used to pretty quickly.

Going back to the first question, everything is precipitated by the calls that come in. The intensity of your training is going to depend on how busy and what type of calls we receive in any given day. That same first day, we had a couple of traffic stops and a child abuse case. But, the most exciting call of the day was, by far, at about three o'clock in the afternoon. We had another "in-progress" call where a known felon had stolen a car the previous day. A zone sergeant saw and stopped him and the entire zone responded "code 3." The occupants of the car got out to run, so we had a foot pursuit going on - officers and canines. All of this is happening and I'm right in the middle of it thinking, "What do you guys need me to do?" I got a chance to book and interview the felon at the city jail. That was eye opening - to talk at length with this guy who's looking at doing some pretty serious time.

TCV: When you get into those situations, does prior training just kick in?

Bocage: The training kicks in. It's immediate - bam, bam, bam. The thing that I was a little apprehensive about is not so much the threat of what's happening in front of us but the process involved and how not to mess

anything up - documentation, writing the report and if I had to take a suspect's statement or a victim's statement that day. In a way, getting everything right is more of a concern for me than the actual crime in progress. That's going to get handled. There's no question about that.

TCV: Do you feel that you have a long way to go?

Bocage: Yeah, I've got a long way to go.

Mahboobi: I know that I have a long way to go - a lot to learn. Like Matt said, I haven't had any doubts about handling the calls and dealing with the issue; it's procedural stuff, it's beyond that. The instinctive response from the training is automatic. But, after that, it's a question of how I did it. There are things that other officers would have done differently and I want to learn all of those things.

I might not be right in trying to solve a problem - I'm not sure it's the way our agency wanted to do it. I don't think I'm doing anything unlawful or wrong, but there are so many procedures and directives on everything - on how we, as an agency, want to handle crimes. There are two binders of about five hundred sheets each - millions of words that I need to memorize. One day, I'll know them all. That's where your doubts come in. That's where the confidence kind of goes down. Am I doing this the way my Training Officer wants me to do it?

So on my days off, I've reviewed as much as I can - all the policies that I've faced already that I didn't quite have the right answers for on day one and day two. I want to make sure that if I handle it again I'll do it the way everyone would want it to be done. What's going to be interesting is if I get the same type of call again. I still might mess it up, because it'll be different. Just because it has the same title doesn't mean it's not a completely different situation.

Bocage: We are trying to figure out exactly how we can take everything that we've learned and everything that we will continue to learn, formulating it into our personalities and the way we choose to handle it. I think every officer is different, and while procedurally we may all do the same things, they all go about it in very different ways. So, it's finding a niche - what works best for us to accomplish the same things. It's the struggle we're working with now.

TCV: Are you encouraged to try different approaches?

Bocage: Absolutely. My FTO is very supportive, very encouraging. Everything that Ramin said is the same for me. I've gone over everything that I can possibly think of. I mean, hours of studying since we got off last shift and I feel like I still don't really know anything. I'm working on mental preparation, visualization. When we get in the car Saturday morning at about 6:45 a.m., I want to be mentally prepared, just how I'm going to deal with the car, with the radio. I've gone over a few different role-playing scenarios in my head as to how we're

going to proceed with certain calls. We're completely dependent upon our FTO. I'm really grateful that I have Officer Crandall as my FTO, because he's going to show me the way and I'm happy with what I've seen.

Mahboobi: The way that we're evaluated in the sense of progress is on how we handled a call compared to a solo officer. The way we're graded is based on how they would have handled it, how much time would they have taken to be able to solve the issue, did they cover all of the material that they needed to cover, and did they hit all the information that they needed. Compared to a solo officer, I'm nowhere near that level yet. I need a lot of help in these calls, making all the right decisions and getting all the right information, asking the right questions, that alone is a huge challenge.

It's going to take a long time to know exactly what I need to do before I am even at the scene. I have an idea, but there's so much that I can overlook in one single call. I show up and it takes me three times the amount of time of an experienced officer. The FTO is there to help you see how you could have achieved the result in a better way and to make sure that you're prepared to know exactly what you need immediately. I'm stumbling through the calls. I'm nowhere near having my own style.

It's still so new to me, even though we've spent all this time training. It's a completely different type of training out there handling the real deal. I know Matt is probably doing a great job, but even so, I think I can speak for both of

Crunch Time

us - we're not at that level. We've got a long way to go, but there's been a lot of support from all the other officers that are there. A lot of cops come up and ask us how it's going, and how our first week has been.

Bocage: We just smile.

Mahboobi: We're looking at them and thinking, "Holy Crap! This is really something," and they're laughing like, "I know, I was there, man."

Bocage: Stock up on headache meds and antacids is what I've been told.

Mahboobi: They are encouraging saying, "Hey, we were there, it's overwhelming but you'll get through it." And that's comforting, because sometimes you feel like, "Man, I must be the worst cop who ever showed up to Day One because I feel so unprepared." Yet, it's how it is. You've just got to stick with it. I'm confident to go back to work, but I know I'll stumble all over myself all over again. As much as I've reviewed all of those directives and thought that they would help me and I've studied what I thought I should have focused on a little more, there's still another book I've yet to open.

Bocage: Exactly.

TCV: Are you enjoying this experience?

Bocage: Yes. It is fantastic. It really is. There have been a lot of highs and some lows. Despite the anxiety, the difficulty and what's expected of us, there's no doubt in my mind that I made the right decision.

Mahboobi: Without a doubt. It's a very serious job, and it's very stressful already, but without a doubt it's the best career out there. I wouldn't trade this hell I'm going through for anything else. I went home feeling like an idiot - to put it bluntly - but I couldn't wait to go back to work the next day. It's exciting.

Bocage: I slept three hours the night before our first day. I went to bed about 1:00 a.m., got up at four, and I was just burning adrenaline all day long, I wound up working 17 hours that day - five hours of overtime. I got home at about 12:30 a.m., didn't go back to sleep until about one-ish, and then I got up at four again, and worked two hours overtime that day. I was drop-dead exhausted after two days but I couldn't stop talking all day, I could not shut up, I was just so excited. Everybody knew exactly what we went through, and how much fun we were having, and how lost I was.

Mahboobi: I'm looking at my days off as not enough time to study for my next shift. There's just so much - penal codes, vehicle codes, procedures, directives, report writing, and the list goes on. I need to learn more. Review, review, review! Learn, learn, and learn! But, I can't wait to go back to work. My days off are too short yet too long between the excitement and the love I have for the job and the desire to conquer this training and be out there on my own.

This is everything I've wanted it to be so far. It's going to be hard and stressful, but this is the most stressful part. You know you're going to make it, but you don't know. You've got to prove it. This is the first time in my life that I've been this excited to go to work. From what I hear, I better get used to the feeling. I've never had so many people training me, so many different instructors and trainers. The one thing they've all agreed on is that they love coming to work every day. It's been that way for me ever since I signed up and got hired. That's what's beautiful about this career.

Bocage: Yeah. We are in a pursuit of experience. I've never wanted experience so bad in my entire life. Just to get that experience is all I think about.

INTERVIEW WITH
Matthew Snelson

TCV: Has your experience met prior expectations?

Snelson: I would say that it met my expectations in a lot of respects. There's a lot of multitasking once you really start getting out there. In the first two days, I wasn't even driving. I was just sitting in the passenger seat, and there was already a lot of information just from there. The last two days of my first week, I started driving, so now, yeah, a huge dynamic. You got your computer screen, but you don't want to be looking at that while you're driving, so you've got to wait until you get to a light or something to get information. You're trying to listen to the radio not only for your call sign and where you're being assigned but your zone partner so you know where they are in case they

get in trouble. You're trying to think through different stuff.

We tried to serve some warrants. We were looking for a couple of stolen cars this week that we heard were in the area. There's just a ton of dynamics going. It met my expectations in some respects - it was extremely stressful. The pace definitely picked up, big time. I actually didn't expect the report writing to take me as long as it has. That, I think, is just learning the style, the format and how to get the information that's needed for the district attorney. Since the last time we talked, one of the days, in our in-house, before we started on the street, we went to the district attorney's office and watched one of the sergeants from our department take the cases over from the night before. It was interesting to see how leaving things out or putting things in to that report made a huge difference. Whether it was done or not in real life, that report was all they had to go on. Just a lot, a ton of multitasking, and just feels like my brain's been running at 120 mph.

TCV: After four long days of duty, what will you do on your days off?

Snelson: I need them. It was a long week. Just for my wife and I. My wife teaches, and it'll give us some time to connect. Really, on those four days, at least right now, we weren't able to see each other much. Maybe a half hour or an hour where I'd come home, eat dinner, and then go to bed. There are some things that I have to buy this week, knowing now what I need to get. I have a test next week that I need to study for. I think we're tested every week throughout the FTO.

TCV: A written test?

Snelson: A written test, yeah. I need to prepare for that. We took tests all the time in the academy, but the department also needs to make sure that we know what we're doing. You've got to know when you can go into somebody's house, when you can't, when you can detain somebody, when you can't. These four days are not only to study for the written test, but also areas that I already see as weaknesses. Studying radio codes and making sure that I just know those off the top of my head. Radio codes, penal codes, making sure you really know the elements inside and out for a crime. When you walk in and meet with somebody, they're going to tell you what happened and you have to be able to pick the bullets that make up the crime; we call them the elements. This week, I'll probably be studying those things, getting my stuff in order. Now I think I have a perspective of what a workweek looks like.

TCV: When you are in uniform and riding in a marked car, is there a difference in the way that the public looks at you?

Snelson: It's different. You can definitely tell when people are watching. I can see in my rearview mirror whenever we get on a road, everybody starts doing the speed limit, which I did too. We got on the freeway the other day and a car was merging from the right. We were about even so I started to slow down, and my FTO says, "No. Don't slow down, because he's going to see a cop car and nobody wants a cop behind them." It is

different. I don't feel different, that's what's weird.

TCV: Is that a process for you, or is it just something that happens immediately?

Snelson: I think some of it is, they talked about command presence. You definitely have to be a little bit different when you have that uniform on. People recognize that authority from that uniform, and you have to own that. We went to a residence yesterday to check on a person's welfare. People hadn't seen them for two weeks and no one was answering the door. I knocked on the door and said, "Fremont Police, we need you to open up," did it three times. I almost didn't do it the third time. We were going to break the deadbolt but about mid-sentence, the guy goes, "Alright! Alright!"

He comes and answers the door, and now it's not just one guy, there are two other guys behind him. At that point, his response is - not because it's me but because it's my uniform - "Whoa, whoa, what's the deal?" I've got three guys inside, and we're in the house taking control. That has to happen. You have to be there to take control. I think the uniform has an effect on people and I think that you also have to control that. You don't want to abuse that, but at the same time it's part of your job.

TCV: Who's your FTO?

Snelson: Officer Quimson.

TCV: How much does he let you do?

Snelson: I was eased into it. Matt and Ramin just happened to get some crazy calls right off the bat. A lot of it is that. It's what call is going to come out. My first day driving, we're out looking for a stolen vehicle. If I find this car and this guy is the person that we think is driving the car - he's had some issues - we can expect some resistance. If I find him - we're rolling out of the police department at 7 a.m. - and see him at 7:05, this is my first day in the car and I'm possibly in a car pursuit! You've got to take all of that into consideration. I think Officer Quimson did a very good job of easing me into things. The first two days, I drove around and got to see him make traffic stops. I would walk up on the passenger side and observe him, listen to what he was doing, watch how he parked his car.

He would hand things off to me. We ran into a traffic collision right off the bat on the first day and he took control of the two people, got them out of harm's way, set his car up to block the intersection to protect the cars. When we got to the side, he got their driver's licenses and handed them to me and told me to "run them." That's the first time I've ever run anything, so I'm thinking about how I'm going to talk to radio, what channel do I go to. I think he did a good job just on the first two days, giving me some easy stuff to ease me in to it. By the second day, I took a few more lead roles in talking to people. I took a family dispute, an argument. Some of those things, I bumbled pretty good, but you've got to learn somehow.

By day three and day four, I was taking a whole lot more of the lead. I was doing the traffic pullovers, I was the one talking, I was talking on the radio a lot more. Officer Quimson did some of the computer work, so that I didn't have to deal with it so much on the first day, but I really wanted to get used to doing it, too. So when I'd get to a light I'd try to do it like I will in the future. I had much more of an easing process than I think Matt and Ramin did. A lot of that was just circumstance.

TCV: Do you feel that the prior training that you received was adequate? When you get into pressure situations, do you feel that the training sort of takes over, and in a way, you go into automatic pilot?

Snelson: Yeah some. I made a few mistakes this week on stuff that I was trained in just from the pressure. I look back and wonder what I was thinking - I know not to do that. I think some of that is just the stress and because there are so many things going on in your head at one time, you have to be conscious of everything that you're doing. A police officer has the power to take someone's freedom from them, even with a detention you are not free to leave right now until I figure out if there is a crime involved here. That's a huge responsibility that carries a lot of civil liability if you do something wrong there. So you're worried about that.

You're thinking about going into somebody's house wrong. You have to have probable cause to get in there. You're worried about all of those interactions. The biggest concern is officer safety. I don't want to get myself or my FTO hurt. There are a lot of things going on. I feel like I got a lot of good training in academy, and now it's just trying to fit it all together in a real life situation. We did scenarios at academy and scenarios are this nice, sterile environment. I actually considered myself a pretty good mediator between people, in academy. It's not hard for me to talk to people. Yet, my first family dispute I just got all jacked up in my mind. Some of it is the adrenaline, and you just start to get that tunnel vision - there's no autopilot yet. I think that comes later on. However, a lot of people have said that sometimes that autopilot is what gets you in trouble.

TCV: After the four days on the streets, are you enjoying yourself?

Snelson: I am. But, there are times. Wednesday night I was not enjoying myself. We took a burglary report. Another officer had been assigned a burglary report, and my FTO said that we would take that for training which was good because you want to take every report you can possibly take while you're in training. I don't want to get out on the street and have to take a burglary report when I've never taken a burglary report before. We went to this business and it turns out that the guy had entered through one business, and then they went through a wall and into the next business. That's not one burglary report, it's two. Two separate ones. Not only was I writing my first burglary report, but I was writing my first two burglary reports at the same

time. The way that Sacramento does their reports is completely different from how Fremont does it. I'm kind of going through this learning process of just doing it. I ended up working late on those.

TCV: Were you prepared for the amount of paperwork involved with police work?

Snelson: I knew that I would be writing a lot of reports. I didn't know that I would be this slow at it right now. My wife and I made a huge sacrifice with me being in Sacramento four days a week during my academy training. I thought when I got back to Fremont that we'd see each other more. The last four days have proven that, at least right now while I'm in training, while I'm learning how to do these things, I'm putting many more hours in than I thought I would. Some of that should have been expected, but I think I was just surprised by that. Because my day shift starts early, I try to go to bed around 8:30 or 9 p.m. and I'm waking up at 4:30 a.m. Most of the shifts are long, like last night was probably my lightest night and I got off at 7 p.m. The window is just pretty small.

TCV: Did you feel prepared for the communication part of policework?

Snelson: You have to report on paper everything that you're going to do because in the end, the point is to convict criminals and to protect the city and myself from liability. You have to document things you do. I knew that, I just didn't think I was going to be that slow about it.

TCV: Looking to the future, what do you expect from your next shift, do you see a gradual increase in confidence or maybe this kind of up and down for maybe the next month or two?

Snelson: I think it's going to go longer than a month or two. Last night, my FTO did a pretty good job of debriefing the week at the end of our shift. At about seven o'clock we sat down and talked about what kind of stuff I needed to study for next week and then talked about the week. I think he's 11 or 14 years on the force and he said that there are plenty of days where, he'll either have a good day or a bad day, he's just on or off. Within the shift, he might have eight great hours of police work, but maybe for two of them he'll wonder where his head was.

I think it's expected that you're always going to have highs and lows. It's just learning to manage that so that your lows aren't endangering yourself, any other officers, the public, and your lows aren't messing up your basic fundamental job - to protect the peace, and to fight crime. I expect my confidence level to slowly rise. My FTO started me off this week with some car stops. That was good because I have to communicate with people, I have to drive the car, activate the lights, do the radio, manage traffic around me and get to that vehicle. My first traffic stop was okay, because I got behind the car and they were at a red light. When the light turned green, I made the call, they pulled over and it went smoothly. My second car stop didn't go so well. I was driving past the car in a residential neighborhood and it had no plates. I got too jacked up and inside I thought, "No plates! That might be a stolen car, or..." and my brain starts spinning. I got too "amped" up. A lot of it is just learning to react in a calm and measured response.

After I messed up that car stop I didn't want to make another car stop because you think you're terrible at it. But inside, you also know that you have to do it again and again to get that confidence. 10, 20, 30 more down the line, I'm going to be able to say that I know how to get to the vehicle; I know how to put the radio traffic out and all of these things. I felt the same thing with the family argument call. I walked out of there thinking that I didn't ever want to do another one of those but at the same time I need to volunteer for another ten. When I go out on my own, I better not be worried about knowing how to perform in those situations.

TCV: How does your wife feel about this?

Snelson: I think she's been doing really well. I think that this week was a good learning week for us because we finally got to see what a week of actually working looked like. I was there pretty late, and I wasn't sure if I could use the city phone to call home real quick and say that I was working late, so she was pretty mad about that, about not getting called. I would be too. I explained that I wasn't sure if I could make that call and then I found out that I could. Since then, that's helped a lot, just communication.

Everything breaks down to communication I think. She's doing really well with it.

Our understanding and expectations are a little more realistic after those first four days. I was sitting there Wednesday night wishing I was home with my wife instead of writing these burglary reports, but they had to get done, I've got to put the long hours in now to learn how to do this stuff, and I'll get faster and better at it and more confident.

Interim Report

Interview with
Matthew Bocage

TCV: Do you feel more confident than the last time we met?

Bocage: I think that there's no question that I feel much better sitting here today than I did two weeks ago. Just the comfort level, operating the radio, listening for the codes, the right call signs, that sort of thing. However, I am far from where I want to be at this point, there's no doubt about it.

TCV: Do you feel as though you are part of the force?

Bocage: I feel fully embraced. My zone partners and shift partners, everybody's senior to me but I feel like everybody's at least done a little part in taking me under their wing. Everybody has been very supportive.

TCV: Do you feel a change in your relationships with people?

Bocage: That started, I think, the moment I was hired but it has definitely evolved to the point now where I'm very conscious of the things that I do, decisions I make off duty. On duty, there's no question as to the decisions.

TCV: As time goes on and you recede more from the experience in Sacramento [Academy Training], how does that feel?

Bocage: Sacramento seems like such a long time ago now. Everything I have now is built on my training in Sacramento.

TCV: When we last spoke, there were a lot of ups and downs in terms of how you felt about all of this. Is that leveling off?

Bocage: It has, to a certain degree. There are still spikes, but I don't think that the peaks and valleys are quite as extreme as they were.

TCV: Do you still have the same enthusiasm?

Bocage: There's no question about it. The more confidence I gain, the more excited I become. The ultimate goal is to be in the car alone. That first day, to me, is going to be the most exciting day.

Interview with
Matthew Snelson

TCV: Are you starting to feel more confident?

Snelson: I'm still taking a lot of new reports. One of the goals of the field training program is to get you exposed to as much as possible so that while you're in training and have a trainer next to you; you can ask questions and deal with things that are new. I would say that the stress level hasn't changed because I'm still trying to grasp multi-tasking, and I don't see that going away anytime soon. There are just so many things going on. It seems like when you get a little bit confident on something, then you're going to get a call that you've never done before. You try to remain competent, you try to revert to your training and what you've been taught to do.

These last couple of days I'm feeling much more confident on our report writing system, more comfortable with the keys, learning how to access that and how to search in different databases for information whether you're running somebody's driver's license or registration, something like that. Accessing information and writing reports has gotten a little bit easier. There's still a ton to learn, especially on the accessing of information stuff.

TCV: Your Sacramento training is receding in time. Do you feel a sense of transition?

Snelson: Definitely. We have automated report writing; our report writing is condensed but thorough. I've been pretty happy with the changes I've had to make here because every change seems logical.

TCV: Are you being treated well by fellow officers?

Snelson: Everybody, bar none, is very friendly, very encouraging. I felt like part of the team, almost right off the bat.

Interview with Ramin Mahboobi

TCV: Are you feeling more confident at this point?

Mahboobi: I do feel a progression, thats the good news. My confidence is growing. Each day this week, I felt more comfortable with what I was going to face that day. I keep learning alternate ways to handle any given situation. Confidence is definitely rising but I'm not going to sit here and act as if I don't realize that I still have a long way to go.

TCV: As your Sacramento experience recedes in time, how do you feel about it?

Mahboobi: Here's how I look at it. What I got from Sacramento, what I received there, I still believe was phenomenal training; it was a fantastic police academy. Those are my roots. What it did was set a foundation for what I'm learning now. I'm bringing my Sacramento training with me every day.

TCV: Do you sense a change in yourself; how you view things?

Mahboobi: Yes. It's a natural thing. I feel this greater responsibility that I'm carrying with me off duty just as well as when I am on duty. For example, the other day I was in a movie theater - it was just yesterday - I'm watching a movie and there are people behind me, talking over it. There was an argument between the person directly behind me and the person behind him. What am I going to do? I want to be a good witness and at the same time, I want to make sure that no one gets hurt over this nonsense. I talked to my buddy, who was watching the film; he had no clue any of it was going on.

TCV: Among your circle of friends, the people you know well, is there a distance now?

Mahboobi: With my close circle of friends, I have not noticed any distance. They've known for a long time that this was my career choice. I have a strong desire to be here; never for any other profession.

Moving to Swing Shift

Officers Matthew Bocage, Ramin Mahboobi and Matthew Snelson have been on patrol under the supervision of a Field Training Officer (FTO) for approximately five weeks. They will soon trade the day shift for a swing shift that begins in the late afternoon and extends through nighttime hours. All expect to see the city in a different way, but expressed the same enthusiasm as when they first began patrol duties. TCV was able to speak briefly with Matthew Snelson and Ramin (Matthew Bocage was unavailable) as they look forward to a new FTO and patrol of different hours.

Five weeks is enough time for some memorable moments and both officers related an incident that stands out at the present time. Ramin began by recounting an incident that began as a routine call to investigate a "suspicious vehicle" parked in a "no parking, no trespassing" residential area. Upon arrival on the scene, it was discovered that two adults, male and female, were sleeping in the car.

Mahboobi: The male doesn't want to ID himself. We do ID him, no problem, and he is on probation with a search clause. We search the car and recovered marijuana and a stolen firearm from a burglary that happened in Fremont in June. I am going to follow up on this to find out how he acquired the gun - whether he acquired the gun from the person who committed the burglary or if he was the burglar. He was on probation for selling marijuana, so obviously this didn't help him with his probation! Now we have a stolen firearm on him as well. Luckily, the gun was unloaded. The man tried to deny knowledge of the gun, but knew it was unloaded and claimed he didn't have any bullets for it. He obviously knew the gun was in the car and in his possession. I will remember this case since it could have been just someone who fell asleep in the car with a very simple explanation. Our job is to check and make sure everyone is okay. We find that the guy is lying, a drug dealer and has a gun in the car! There was a stolen stereo in the trunk that the female swore wasn't hers and knew nothing about and later claimed was for her car. She was the registered owner of the car so it turns out that she was in possession of stolen property. I learned a lot with this case.

This is one of the most dangerous times in this job. When approaching vehicles, the person inside the car can be doing many things - some that can be life-threatening to an officer. The first five seconds of a stop is probably the most dangerous time - the approach - identifying who is in the car, what are their actions.

In this particular case, the windows were fogged up and I couldn't see anything until I was right up next to the car. If this guy had been awake with a loaded gun, things might have turned out much differently!

Snelson: For me, it is seeing how things unfold. You can go on a simple call or a routine stop and end up with something that is definitely not routine. We got into our first big case where we ended up arresting three parolees a while back. A warrant check ended with the discovery of a lot of marijuana plants in the back of his truck and about 186 grams of marijuana on his person. After three hours of searching and photographing his car, we found a Cannabis Buyers Club card and he says, "Oh yeah, I'm a Cannabis Club member." This started out as a misdemeanor arrest warrant and ended up, after some investigation, turning up five arrest warrants out for this guy.

Another time, I pulled a guy over at 6:45 a.m. and he had no license, no insurance and no registration. We thumb printed him and took his picture to prove that this was the person we stopped and cited him. He had to walk since he didn't have a license to drive. Upon further investigation, we found that the information given did not check out. The guy was wearing a fast food restaurant shirt and said he was on his way to pick up his wife at the restaurant. We went to the restaurant and found him "flipping fries." We arrested him for giving false information and it turns out that he has five aliases in the Fremont system. He had been in jail under a different name. Here, I thought I was stopping a guy for a simple driving infraction!

Mahboobi: Often these guys know how to avoid giving information. When questioning someone, another officer heard the name over the radio and recognized it and told me that the guy had quite a few "priors" under a different name. Now all the aliases are linked. The teamwork here is fantastic.

Night Vision

Officers Matthew Snelson, Matthew Bocage and Ramin Mahboobi are now working on the "swing shift" which includes late afternoon, night and early morning hours.

TCV: This shift is something new for you? What are the differences?

Snelson: Sleep was huge! I went from waking up at 4 a.m. to trying to sleep until 12:30 p.m. and going to work from 4 p.m. to 3 a.m. We get off at 3 a.m., but you have to write reports after that. There were a few nights when I got out at 4:30 or 5:00 a.m. This was a change for my wife and I since she is teaching and I get home at 5 a.m. She gets up a couple of hours after I go to bed. She writes notes to me about her day and her classes and I now write her notes about my "day."

The people we deal with have changed a ton - a completely different populace! During the day we dealt with your normal average citizen. You might be going to some problem calls like a family fight but at night, there are more family fights and more people under the influence or have been drinking. They have been home for awhile. You definitely see a different side of life at night.

Bocage: During the day shift, I would get on at 6 a.m. and usually have a chance to "warm up" and then the calls would start picking up during the

morning. Now, we have a briefing at 4:30 a.m. and things are already hot - very, very active. There are usually several calls waiting. We are being dispatched constantly; right out of the gate. You are hitting the ground running on this shift. As soon as the sun goes down, everything is moving.

Snelson: There are traffic pattern changes too. During the day there is so much more traffic on the roads that you have to be very conscious of how you are driving - you have to be aware at any time - but at night there are far less people out so when we need to get to a call quickly, the traffic is much lighter.

TCV: Are the calls different in scope or just more numerous?

Bocage: Loud music and disturbance calls are numerous. There are more nightlife activities getting out of control like bar fights. That is different.

Mahboobi: We are in the same zone and working the same hours so we see each other more now. If there is an in-progress call, we will probably see each other since our FTO's (Field Training Officers) will want us to get the experience. We are seeing new things now. I notice a lot more in-progress calls, so I am not just showing up to take a report with no suspect or suspect description. I am showing up with the suspect there. There is a whole different approach and mindset. Day shift has its share of in-progress calls too, but in the short time I have been on swing shift, there have been a lot more in-progress calls.

We will probably see a lot more of each other at these calls. It's good to see a friend and see the same look in his eyes reflecting the same questions I have about handling the call.

Snelson: When we have a music disturbance or loud party call, a "BOL" is broadcast on the radio which means "Be On the Lookout." The department used to dispatch an officer to answer the call, but now, because of staffing levels, we are told of the problem and if we happen to be in the area, can deal with it.

Mahboobi: Once we hit the streets at 4 p.m., there are calls waiting, so we are already down in work. As we get out of briefing, get in the car and log on, within the first 30 seconds there is a call. From then on, it is just call to call to call. I don't really notice a peak of activity. It is like you are in a hole and you are trying to get out. Until at least 11 p.m. or midnight, we are handling calls continuously and then it seems like, although calls are still coming in, we start to have the staffing to handle the calls. It begins to balance out. By around 1 a.m., it begins to slow down.

Snelson: We are very conscious of our zone partners since many calls translate to

reports. If you happen to get a big case that requires a lot of paperwork, it takes you out of the zone for a period of time and creates a heavier load for the others. You are trying to do all you can for the case but at the same time you want to support your partners in the zone. It is a tough juggling act.

TCV: Have you had any significantly new experiences?

Bocage: Yesterday was my first court testimony in a felony case. It went pretty well. This was just a preliminary hearing to decide whether there was enough evidence to take the case further. Along the same line, now that we are in our sixth week, I am seeing a lot of the cases that I started, come back with convictions. We get disposition forms that let us know what happened to the person we arrested. We are coming full circle seeing the punishment that is given to these people.

TCV: Did you feel prepared for your court appearance?

Bocage: I felt well prepared - our academy training prepares us. The deputy district attorney also prepared me well. I was a little nervous, but once I settled in, it was okay. You just testify to what you saw and heard - what is in your report. It is important to have good notes since court appearances are often many weeks after the arrest and we have to rely on our reports. This appearance helped me to understand what I should include in my reports.

Snelson: I watched the court testimony of Matt and Officer Ehling and I was impressed by how they handled themselves. They looked confident even though I am sure they were nervous inside. It was interesting to watch them and see the prosecutor ask questions and then the defense attorney take his turn. There were two defense attorneys in this case, so you have to go through two different sets of questions.

Bocage: It was a great experience. You can see the defense attorney taking notes while the prosecutor is asking questions. You want to look as competent as possible, telling the truth, being professional and courteous. I had to recall a lot from my memory and consult my notes. The biggest lesson of all is to know what needs to be in my reports to be prepared for testimony in court.

Snelson: That is supposed to be the end result of our work. If you arrest somebody, you want them to be put in jail for the crime.

Mahboobi: The prosecution of criminals is what validates our work as a police officer.

TCV: What is the primary operational difference when patrolling on the swing shift?

Bocage: I am still having a hard time adjusting to what happens at night; even something like a car stop. There is enough going on in the daytime; now you have to worry about - there are more buttons you have to push on the display panel - lighting up the car in front of you with the spotlight just to see what is going on. It will be a couple of weeks until I am comfortable. I had a code 3, lights and siren, last night and I didn't feel comfortable.

Snelson: When you are trying to get to something quickly, street signs are harder now and numbers are very difficult. A lot of places don't have numbers on their houses or they are not easily read. You may be driving along and suddenly the numbers jump 200 digits and find yourself "on top" of the house you are looking for. That is not where you want to be. It is best to stop before the house.

Mahboobi: We want to have the advantage when we arrive, but if we stumble across the place and the next thing we know, we are right at their front yard, we have lost our advantage. You lose the element of surprise. It is a new challenge!

Bocage: We have resources to help us locate a call. We are given some street direction but that just gets you to the street.

Snelson: The other thing I am struggling with is coming to the scene as a cover officer. The primary officer has already made contact and they may be standing in the dark. I need to turn my headlights off as I approach so I don't destroy their night vision. Light management is the package we have added. This is when to add light, when not to add light. You don't want to shine a flashlight behind another officer because that silhouette's him. Light management is huge!

Bocage: The things you can readily see on the day shift often cannot be seen easily at night. The level of danger escalates because of this.

TCV: Are procedures more automatic now or do you still find yourself missing parts of a protocol?

Mahboobi: With repetition, many things are now automatic. However, depending on the situation, I might miss something. It seems that just as we begin to get an understanding of our role, they change the rules on you. Now, we are working in the dark and there are more things to do. It adds more tasks to the same game. There are many steps to take even before we get out of the car. This will improve with time. Every day we go home, we go home wiser. We just need to do it over and over again.

Feeling the Pulse

Fremont Police Department rookies, Matthew Bocage, Ramin Mahboobi and Matthew Snelson have been working on the "swing shift" (4 p.m. - 3 a.m.) for the past several weeks and relate some of their thoughts and experiences.

TCV: Can you single out an interesting learning experience or incident that you have been called to recently?

Bocage: There was an incident in Niles where we had several hundred youths over at Munoz Hall who got out of hand at a party. It started out as a disturbance which escalated into a fight, and then into a 'shots fired' call, so every cop in the city made their way down there; we had BART police and Union City out there helping us.

It went pretty well; the goal in a situation like that is to get the crowd dispersed as safely as possible. We had some squad sergeants on hand, and formed skirmish lines; basically all the tactical things that I learned about in the academy. We were just forcing the crowd back, out to all the main outlets to Mission Blvd as best as we could. It was a little chaotic, a little hectic, but it went smoothly. Under the circumstances, we organized well, communication was good, and we managed to disperse the crowd in a reasonable amount of time without anyone getting hurt.

After we got the crowd moving, we went to the Mission/Niles intersection, anticipating that there would be a lot of foot and vehicle traffic. We stayed posted there to make sure that they didn't all get back together and cause havoc, or do any looting to the businesses there.

TCV: Did you feel hostility?

Bocage: There was a lot of confusion and it was hostile at first. This crowd had been together a long time, and some were intoxicated. But I think we had a strong enough show of force that we quelled anything that may have happened. There were dozens of officers on the scene within minutes. We had our lethal and non-lethal weapons deployed. We were able to keep them from getting an attitude with us, but we were ready for anything that was going to happen. The ultimate goal was just to get the crowd to leave.

TCV: It all clicked in with the training you've had?

Bocage: Absolutely. It all coincided with what we've been taught about crowd control. It went directly from an academic level to being applied in the street in a seamless fashion. I was quite impressed with it, actually. It became real and practical, with everyone running around, car loads of people going here and there. It's good to see the coordination between the outside agencies as well. Collectively, I think we did a real good job.

TCV: Officer Mahboobi, what has been your experience these last couple of weeks?

Mahboobi: We've had a lot of in-progress calls. The difference between the swing shift and the day shift has been a higher pace. As soon as we get out of briefing and hit the streets, there's a lot of stuff waiting for us. You just immediately jump right into your shift. I've been experiencing a wider variety of calls.

I missed the Niles incident, because earlier in the evening there were seven individuals, all juveniles, who had been driving around, jumped out of their car and beat up another juvenile and robbed him. This is something that they had done a few times in the city and we had received a call from another victim who described the vehicle. Another officer, Officer Gaches, stopped the vehicle, and I took the report from the victim, who identified the stopped vehicle. So we ended up making the arrest on all seven individuals.

Once we were on the scene, I learned that my FTO (Field Training Officer), Officer Hummel recognized the vehicle description from a prior case in the same type of incident, so we then knew that these juveniles had done this in our city several times before. We contacted prior victims, to get identification from

them as well. It took a long time to go through and solve these prior cases, but we were able to take all seven into custody, book them, and get them to juvenile hall.

I transported them to Juvenile Hall in San Leandro, and since it was a Saturday, they stayed there until Monday, when they could see a judge. We notified their parents to let them know that they were being detained. There are similarities between juveniles and the adult system, but there are special needs involved, such as the requirement to separate them from adults in a jail facility. Also, they are charged differently than adults, because they end up in a rehabilitation program. A lot of writing was involved in the reports.

The whole process took about four or five hours, so I missed that whole incident in Niles, but I learned how much goes into one arrest. I got to see the difference between dealing with juveniles, as opposed to adults. All seven of them were arrested for robbery. It was a good case.

TCV: How do you handle a large group and maintain control?

Mahboobi: Officer Gaches, who did the initial traffic stop on the vehicle, did a great job; he put out the information and requested a cover unit. He was unable to see exactly how many people were in the car, but he could see about six of them, so he called the other officer to meet him. He and the other officer handled the traffic stop while I took the report from the victim. We had not even been sure that we would find the vehicle, and then the report came on the radio that Officer Gaches had it.

Since he called for a cover unit, we had the numbers present to take total control of all seven suspects. Luckily, when it was only two officers on the initial traffic stop, none of them made an effort to run for it, even though given the circumstances and location where they were, I don't think they would have gotten far, and they were smart enough not to try.

We're trained to make those stops when we're in the advantage, and Officer Gaches did a good job. He didn't pull the car over immediately, but waited until he had his cover unit and made the stop in a strategic area. By the time I showed up, the suspects were all lined up on the curb, and the two officers on the scene (Officers Gaches and Hernandez) had the situation going to their advantage.

I talked with Officer Gaches later on, and he told me what had been going through his mind. This is exactly how we've been trained to look at the situation and make decisions. You have to process that really quickly. You have to think about how many (suspects) am I dealing with? How close is my cover? You can dictate when to turn your lights on, and you can foresee where you're going to stop them.

TCV: What's been noteworthy on your shift, Matt?

Snelson: We got into a pursuit of a stolen vehicle. We were two blocks away when the call came and tried to get there in time to put spike strips down in the road, but the car was on top of us too fast, so we just blocked the intersection so that traffic wouldn't get "T-boned" (broadside) as he went through. He went down Grimmer and Blacow at about 75 mph, running the red light. We had been on Grimmer and Carol at the time. He got on the freeway going south.

This was my first pursuit, and I was the third car in. When I went to make a U-turn on Grimmer, I didn't get on it hard enough, so I was about 100 yards behind him by the time he blew the red light. I couldn't go through the light at a comfortable speed. Everyone else's head is turned, watching him, and I didn't want to T-bone anyone, so I was out of the pursuit before it even started. That was a learning experience.

We still tried catching up to him. We got on the freeway doing 90 mph, and our sergeant stopped the pursuit. We found out that the guy had stolen a plate from another Lexus, which was almost identical to the one he was driving. There was another pursuit with the same suspects and the CHP caught up with them in San Jose.

There was another pursuit in Hayward last night of four suspects and one of them was wanted for murder. Hayward PD hit the car and took out the rear end. We had been "snaring" the area, and had every section covered, looking for the vehicle for two hours. The sergeant had just called to tell us to end the snare when one of our lieutenants picked up the car, and the pursuit was on.

TCV: Have you used the tasers yet?

Mahboobi: No, but we handled a bar fight with the potential of use. There wasn't even a call put out; we were cruising by the area. We got near the bar, and we heard a commotion. There was a mob of people outside, and we're wondering 'what's going on?' We lit it up, called it in: "fight in progress, tasers deployed." People knew what we had, and right away the crowd started to disperse. One instigator almost got it, and I was ready to do it! But he backed off just in time. If he had continued, he would have gotten zapped.

TCV: So all the media coverage of the tasers has had an effect.

Mahboobi: We had a parolee last night who was arguing with his girlfriend. He's big time, he's been in Pelican Bay. He's been in prison for 27 years, a big time gang member. He started listing all the prisons he's been in, and I stopped him after counting 10. One of our cover officers pulled out a taser, so this guy put on a plaid jacket, thinking maybe it would protect him from it. He was getting amped up, and I thought we were going to go rounds with him, but he backed off.

Snelson: We had an emotionally disturbed individual in the Kaiser parking lot. The call said it was a suspicious vehicle. The security had approached him and shone a flashlight into his car and saw a gun on the front seat. So they called us, and we were the third unit on the scene. The guy tried to leave, but we surrounded him. Next thing you know, half the cops in the city are on the scene, and it turned into a barricaded subject stand-off situation. He had knives, and he was brandishing them, pretending to shave and putting the knife up to his throat, that sort of thing. It was by far the most intense situation I've been in so far. We wound up blowing his windows out with a .45 bean bag gun, and then pretty much rushed him. We tazed him, and used pepper ball grounds to help get him in compliance.

TCV: What about light management? Are you getting better at it?

Bocage: I'm getting a little better, still doing some things wrong, though. My last shift I was holding my flashlight in my dominant hand, which is a big no-no, and I got written up. You actually want to have it in your non-dominant hand, so that you can draw your weapon quickly.

Mahboobi: There are a lot of important things. As your approach to cover another officer, you have to shut off your lights so that you're not putting a big, bright backdrop on him, especially if he's approaching a car. I'm getting better about light management. It's a matter of repetition. Now I need to remember to recharge my flashlight, before I get in trouble for having no light! I have explained the weak light to my FTO by saying 'I'm just trying to be on stealth, sir!'

It's a lot of fun learning, and I've been improving. Now that we're on a nighttime shift, it's routine. The more exposure you have to every type of situation, it becomes secondhand.

TCV: What about you, Matt?

Bocage: This week went much better. I'm still working on getting out of the car faster, on traffic stops. It's harder to see what you're trying to call out at night, and there are more lights to turn on and deal with, so everything seems to happen a little bit quicker. There have been incidents where people have been trained to storm the police car as soon as it stops, because they know that officers take too long to get out of the car at first. So it's a critical thing to get out quickly.

Now I'm enjoying the night scene. I'm able to catch people speeding at night, because they don't know you're a police officer, versus during the day, when they can tell. I've gotten some good traffic stops. Last night I stopped some guys who were smoking marijuana in the car while driving. So I stopped them for speeding, and then I was able to turn them in for a little more than that.

I'm starting to wake up better at night now. I've had much more energy this week than I did last time. I got a guy on a DUI who was at 1.7, which is double the legal limit. There were about 14 beer bottles in his car.

Snelson: It's definitely a different clientele [than the day shift].

TCV: Do you feel more like part of the department now?

Snelson: I'm starting to sense how we do things in Fremont a little better. The academy is a more sterile environment, where they're really pushing for officer

safety. And it's stressed in Fremont too, but you can't be this stiff board when you interact with people. There are some contrasts on how we deal with people. The way you stand and interact with people; you have to be able to ebb and flow. When you pull grandma over, it's a lot different than when you pull over, say, four gang members that are flying their colors. I've sensed that I have felt the pulse of Fremont.

I've gotten some real positive interactions with citizens. It's kind of cool to be in a city where the citizens still respect and like the police, which is not the case in many other cities. I had a call from a dad the other night, whose daughter's window got kicked in at the bar fight. He left a message saying thanks for being there for my daughter, and if you need any more information, give me a call. People pull up alongside us and wave "hi," that sort of thing. I feel more a part of the department now but I'm going to be a rookie for a long time.

TCV: How about you, Matt?

Bocage: I would absolutely echo everything he just said. My frame of reference has changed, from when my only experience had been from the academy, and that sterile training. Now I've written about 50 or 60 reports and I've been a cover officer on many more scenes, so that's become my frame of reference. I'm relating to those experiences, rather than to my academy experience to get me through these calls. I'm feeling more comfortable, in control of the calls. We have definitely been

Feeling the Pulse

getting more acceptance by the other officers - and been the butt of their jokes - which is a good thing.

Snelson: The other officers are generally happy to have fresh faces, people who want to be part of the organization. And they're finally getting some additional manpower, which was sorely needed.

Mahboobi: I agree. Having some experience to reference really counts in real life situations. Being able to go back and recall how we handled it last time makes a world of difference to your level of confidence. It's only in those situations that I can say that I feel like I'm a step ahead, and know exactly how I want to go ahead, and control the scene.

Mahboobi: There's times when I'm not as aggressive as I should have been, but once you see it done, you learn that, and the next time you come in with a different approach.

Every situation is different and unique, but it helps to know how you want to solve it. I'm starting to have an idea right off the bat how to get it done effectively. We're big rookies, they should put "R's" on our chests, but every day is a chance to learn and get better. There's a good percentage of the time when I feel like I know what I'm doing, and that feels good.

Snelson: We are in double digits [weeks on the job] now.

A New Set of Challenges

I n this segment, all three officers talk about their past few weeks as they rotate through different departments and work shifts.

Interview with Ramin Mahboobi

TCV: How has your last week been?

Mahboobi: It has been a busy week for me. This week was investigations week. My first day was pretty slow, following up on a lot of cases. The next day was okay with a couple of good cases and interviews. I interviewed children who were victims of crimes and learned a lot from that. Later that day, we had a homicide occur around 4 p.m. It was in progress and the suspect was still "on scene." A page said "all officers return to duty!" Even those who were off duty and on their way home at that point had to report.

I showed up with Detective Sergeant [Dean]Cobet. Our lead homicide detectives were in the middle of things. A command center was set up and we then tried to bring the victim to safety. We knew that we had an armed suspect in an apartment complex. We had the victim transported to Eden Trauma Center but unfortunately, he was pronounced dead at the hospital. There was a standoff with the suspect. I got to see first-hand, one of the most serious situations we can encounter. There are hostages with an armed suspect and a potential for more casualties. There was

the possibility of more than one firearm in the apartment.

In a case like this, it is generally the Special Unit's jurisdiction until there is some resolution. Then the detectives take over the case and do the investigation. We had called out for SWAT who was in charge to control the situation and hopefully prevent further injuries. It was fascinating to see this in operation. You see movies about this sort of thing and have ideas about what goes on. At academy, we studied these scenarios, but to have it happen in front of you is something else!

I thought about all the different scenarios that could transpire. The hostage negotiating team was on scene. We evacuated other apartments and tried to keep curious bystanders out of harm's way. Some people wanted to come into the area because they wanted to go home or see what was going on irrespective of the danger. There were people just walking through the scene without any sense of danger even though there are a lot of police, a SWAT team in full protective gear and big guns and obviously something serious going on.

I did a little bit of everything. I went with the detective who interviewed the victim's wife. It is a very emotional time and you need to be sensitive to their state of mind. You need the facts to determine what has happened and what might happen, but understand that this person is in a traumatic state of mind. I stopped to think about how devastating this must be. The detective and officer talking with her were doing an excellent job. It was overwhelming to see how much is going on. We found other family members and decided to get them away from the chaos so we could interview them in a calm, quiet environment.

Once we found out that the victim was pronounced dead, it was the hardest thing I have seen for the relatives to be informed. Witnessing this was so difficult; it's hard to imagine doing it. It is so hard for both ends.

TCV: Are the police who are holding the perimeter relieved as others come on duty?

Mahboobi: You hold your position. In this case, the suspect would not be able to leave the apartment without greeting an officer. Everyone is at a post until relieved.

At the academy, they taught us that when the situation is stabilized without threats of further violence, time is on your side. You are concerned, but there is nothing saying there is imminent danger. At that point, you want time to go by so the person will wear down and can be talked out.

Mahboobi: In this situation, we were making phone contact with him. We were never at a comfort level to think we could just sit back and wait. Finally, two hostages were released, but the

suspect's wife was still with him. We were constantly going over different scenarios. The hostage negotiator, Officer Crandall, did a great job and when the suspect finally surrendered, the first thing he said was, "Where's Gregg." A personal bond formed between the negotiator and the suspect.

TCV: Are all officers trained in hostage negotiation?

Mahboobi: To some extent, but that is post academy training. We are trained to know how to approach people and when to use different approaches to a situation.

Every shift has an officer designated as "HNT," a hostage negotiator. Most likely we may be the first officer on a scene. Our job is to establish control, balance the situation as much as we can until the advanced resources get to the scene. We have to know how to try to stabilize the situation and get people out of harm's way including a victim.

TCV: When did the detectives start to do their work?

Mahboobi: Once the house was cleared of any further danger. Then the crime scene is "locked down" and the investigators go to work. I authored a search warrant, even though we could have received permission from the wife. All possible items that we want to search for needed to be listed as well as a detailed description of the residence to be searched and the areas to be searched. I called a judge to let him know that I was working on the warrant. It took three hours to fill out the search warrant and then I came by his house a little after midnight and the judge reviewed and signed it. I was told that I was to be in charge of the search. It was a little strange to be telling all these veteran officers what to do! It was amazing how they worked with me. Here I am a rookie and veterans were telling me to "take charge." It's amazing! Every action is documented. Also, everyone involved needed to be interviewed and all this information is put together for legal proceedings.

I came back to work the next day and continued my work on the case. At the same time, I was scheduled to work with the Secret Service so I was involved with that too. This was after five hours sleep! It was very interesting to observe their work.

Back to the homicide investigation and through more reports and briefings where we check out everything that needs to be done so the case is followed up as tightly as possible. There is no chance of anything going undocumented. It is very organized and I was very impressed.

Interview with Matthew Snelson

TCV: Did you feel that returning to the swing shift was a letdown after working on investigations?

Snelson: No, not at all! In my last two weeks on swing shift with Officer [Kevin] Gott, we had one unfortunate incident when we assisted a midnight officer who was tracking down a family of someone killed in a traffic accident. We went to a house to tell the victim's sister about the accident. As far as I know, the accident was just that - the driver was following the speed limit and following all the rules of the road. That was tough!

I had a good time in investigations, but it was fun coming back to swing. When you are on patrol, there is no time to get into things as deeply as investigations. However, when you are on patrol, you are in it - it is happening! Investigations unit is sometimes a bit more removed, but you are able to pick up the ball and run with it and handle things in more depth.

TCV: Does the investigating officer tell the next-of-kin or is a specialist used for this?

Snelson: It is the officer who does this. We want whoever needs to be notified to hear the information from us. We also need to get an ID as well. In this case, there was no identification on the body except a hat that was issued by her place of employment. We had to backtrack to find out who she was. The manager of the business was new and confused her with another employee. We ended up going to another residence first and found ourselves with the named victim answering the door. It turned out that this person roomed with the victim and was able to help identify her.

TCV: Are you trained to talk with survivors?

Snelson: Not really. We become very sensitive to the situation. In this particular instance, the person we were talking to didn't speak English well and we brought another officer in to help communicate. It is hard enough to tell someone their loved one died without having to overcome a language barrier too. This was the second time I have had

A New Set of Challenges

to do this. The first time was a suicide and in that case, I did the notification of the family. Since we talk with people every day, it becomes a matter of sensitivity. It isn't something anyone likes to do. You have to do it - it's part of the job.

TCV: Anything else?

Snelson: I have worked on a lot of accidents. We dealt with the rain for the first time on this shift. I ended up directing traffic at Niles Canyon and Mission for about three hours. The lights went out and it was crazy! 99% of the people do very well, but every once in a while, people are not paying attention even with flares, flashing police lights and I am in the middle of the intersection! It only takes one exception to create an accident. We were trying to stay on our toes.

Another experience this last week was watching the K-9 competition held in the area. There were about 40 dogs competing. One of our officers, Jason Davison and his dog, Kanto, took second place overall. Bobby Davila and his dog, Tuffy, took a few awards as a rookie canine officer.

I am just continuing to learn. The other night was my last shift with Officer Gott, my second Field Training Officer (FTO). My last day, I made a few mistakes and walked away feeling like I wanted one more day so I could end with a good feeling. In my view, it was not a good day. This is an officer that I respect and wanted to leave this part of training on a positive note.

TCV: Have you learned more about light management?

Snelson: Yes! I am much better with that!

TCV: What's next?

Snelson: I have traffic for a week with Officer [Dennis] Madsen. I want experience in writing reports on accidents. Then I go to "mids."

The thing that has really hit me is the amount of discretion we have as police officers. When we are working with people on a situation, the outcome can often depend on how people react and assist with our investigation of what happened. There are instances where something can be viewed in several ways and we have to decide how to approach the circumstances. We had a case where someone hit a fence and left the scene. There were no injuries or anyone else involved. When we found the driver, it could have been written as property damage but his attitude and other circumstances resulted in a citation for hit and run instead.

Officer Gott made a comment that I remember when we were at a traffic accident and had to make a decision of what would be done. A man was driving with a suspended license. We allowed him to take his tools out of the truck before it was towed and impounded since these were his livelihood. We could have impounded the tools in the truck as well. He said that our goal is not to destroy people, rather make them aware of when they are breaking the law.

Interview with Matthew Bocage

TCV: What have the last couple of weeks been like for you?

Bocage: Pretty good. We just finished up our weekend investigations and that was a very profound experience. We had a very, very good time up there. I learned an awful lot. We had our first homicide go down on Wednesday. There was a barricaded subject and hostage situation. That was quite an ordeal. I wasn't actually at the scene like Ramin was, but I got to see how the department responds to this type of crisis situation. It was pretty exciting to see and I got a chance to participate in the investigation.

The suspect had a safe in his house that was seized after a search warrant was obtained. With the assistance of Detective Mark Dang, I was able to get into the safe and see evidence inside. There was some stuff that should be very helpful to the investigation.

TCV: Was this done "by the book"? Was it something that you had learned about now coming to life?

Bocage: We didn't receive much training on background investigation but as far as I could tell, it was extremely by the book. There's a lot of detail that goes on behind the scenes just to make sure that the investigation is ironclad and that we get a good conviction, a good case out of it. They really spare no expense in time or energy to make sure that everything is done by the book. It's pretty exciting.

TCV: Did you write up any of the reports? What were you doing?

Bocage: I wound up documenting the evidence seizure I spoke about earlier in a supplementary report. The thing about the reports is for normal cases, you'll get an original report and then you'll have one or two, sometimes three supplemental reports. Sometimes it's just the original only, depending on what actually happened in your case.

In this case, I wrote the 22nd supplemental report! And, there's more to be done. It's going to be quite a volume when it's all said and done. Great case, though. It was a fantastic training experience. Ramin actually had the opportunity to be at the scene at the time.

TCV: What else were you doing in the investigation unit?

Bocage: I had an opportunity to tie up a lot of loose ends in cases that we had taken from being on patrol. We actually had a chance to finally sit down and close a lot of them, get the final interviews, the final statements from cases that were a week or more old. We had an opportunity to work with the Secret Service, the Department of Treasury, for a couple of days. That was pretty interesting. They were working a case in town so we got a chance to meet a couple of those guys and do some surveillance. It was pretty impressive - pretty unique to see.

TCV: Are the relationships good between the local law enforcement and secret service?

Bocage: Yes, very good. Very cordial. Very professional. A lot of the things that we do are similar. They are all really nice guys. Everyone got along great, there was a lot of joking around.

TCV: You are now finished with swing shift. Are you going to traffic?

Bocage: We finished phase two last week - investigations this past week - and next week, I'll start with traffic. We have a full week of that. That's basically citing moving violations, writing tickets and taking collision reports. Ramin and I will be working the same shift. It should be pretty exciting.

TCV: After working with Investigations, are you interested in pursuing that type of police work?

Bocage: At this point, I can't say that I'm interested in one more than the other. It's very, very different. The pace itself is very different. On patrol, everything is going at one thousand miles per hour - it's very, very fast paced. It's call to call to call. You do have an opportunity to do some follow up on your cases but not to the degree that investigations do.

Investigators have the authority to leave town - we were in San Leandro doing some interviews with a couple of juvenile victims and stuff earlier in the week. They get to go wherever the cases take them, be it out of city, out of county, out of state. They get to follow up all the loose ends. They have the time to be as thorough as they need to be. The pace is definitely different. Sometimes it can be pretty relaxed, pretty slow, other times these guys, they never go home. It's neat to see the contrast between the two. Investigation is absolutely an ambition of mine somewhere down the road. It usually takes a few years to get there. I

definitely see myself there at some point in my career.

TCV: Talking about the paper work, is this more than you expected?

Bocage: I think it's a little bit more. Each agency is different but the degree of documentation that we are responsible for in our agency is pretty significant. You get used to it. There's a lot of documentation involved. It's a good thing. Ultimately, their goal is to get a conviction and have successful prosecution. The degree of documentation definitely helps in that. It's still strikes me to see how much we actually have to write, how much documentation gets done to sustain these cases.

TCV: How do you feel now? Are you feeling a little more confident about these things? Are you getting enough experience under your belt?

Bocage: Confidence is a tricky thing because even though our exposure level increases every week, so do expectations. You have got to keep performing at a higher and higher level to get the same amount of positive feedback. I don't mind the higher expectations, but you need to learn how to eliminate the little things. It's still kind of tough, because we're still only ten or eleven weeks in so it's all good. I'm definitely not complaining. I need to continue to pick it up, I need to continue to learn and perform at increasingly higher rates to enjoy the kudos that I was enjoying earlier on in the program.

TCV: Does it seem like a long time ago when you went to academy?

Bocage: It seems like forever. We graduated at the end of June and it doesn't feel like that happened this year. At the same time, the ten or eleven weeks that we have been in the FTO program seem like nothing. I could probably be in an FTO program for months longer than we're actually supposed to before I actually feel comfortable. I think it's an appropriate amount of time. The learning curve is high, the pace is fast, but I think the goal is to get you as much exposure as possible in a reasonable amount of time. You can't have the training wheels on forever. Eventually, the city needs you. They're paying you to be out there doing a job and that can't have you on a training mode for too long.

TCV: Where do you go from traffic?

Bocage: After traffic I move into the third phase, which will be with Officer [Donn]Tassano, a very experienced, knowledgeable officer. We'll be moving to "mid" shift. The hours will be from 8 p.m. to 7 a.m. We'll basically be in darkness from start to finish.

TCV: Where do you see things going from there? Is that the end of the program or do you go on to something else?

Bocage: After the four weeks with what we call your tertiary FTO, you rotate back to your primary FTO, which in my case would be Officer Gregg Crandall, and you're with him for two weeks. It's no longer a training phase at that point, it's purely an evaluation phase called a shadow phase. They're there, but they're not there. They're in the car for the first week, and then they take an unmarked vehicle out with you for the second week.

The time for leaning on the shoulder of the FTO is pretty much over. At that point you have to rely on your fellow field officers. If you have any questions, you bounce ideas off of them, as you would as a solo patrol officer rather than leaning on your FTO for the answers. The evaluation can be extended in any given phase depending on how your training is going. The little mistakes can add up to a lot.

A New Set of Challenges

A Brief Look at Investigations

TCV has been following three new police officers with the Fremont Police Department: Matthew Bocage, Matthew Snelson and Ramin Mahboobi. Officers Bocage and Mahboobi who have continued training on the swing shift (4 p.m. - 3 a.m.) were unavailable for this session but Matt Snelson recounted his experiences in the last two weeks including a brief look at investigations.

TCV: What has been happening during the last two weeks?

Snelson: I am back on "swing" now, but last week I was with the investigative unit. I worked two days with Crimes Against Property and two with Crimes Against Persons. It was really interesting. I worked with Detective [James] Larkin on the Crimes Against Property to begin and the first day, we served a couple of warrants on a case he has been working on - a person burned their car. It looks like they purchased the car that was a little "over their head" and decided it was smarter to torch it and collect the money from insurance. Detective Larkin was on this pretty much from the beginning. The situation didn't seem right as a stolen vehicle. There were three people involved and we went to their homes to serve search warrants - one outside the City of Fremont.

Shortly after we visited the second door with a search warrant, the suspects called the District Attorney and indicated they wanted to "plea out." They admitted to the crime and wanted Detective Larkin off their back!

TCV: What is the protocol when working within another city?

Snelson: When the search warrant was written, it states that any police officer can serve this warrant. The judge has jurisdiction over California, so when they say that you now have permission to search this house they can give permission outside our city. We let the other police force know that we are there.

In this instance, we requested a uniformed police officer for two reasons. First, it becomes obvious that we are police. We wear our vests, badges and guns, but a full uniform is that much more conspicuous. We need them for presence. Also, if somebody runs, they know all the streets in the area and would take over any pursuit.

This was the second time I went outside Fremont and in the first instance, I was working with Officer [Donald] Martinez who was working a case of someone who was using many different identities. Officer Martinez did a lot of legwork and figured out where this guy was. We went to where he was expected to be and called the local police who provided five officers, and caught this guy hiding in his closet. Although we were in full police uniform, we contacted the local police because they know the area.

TCV: There must also be the courtesy of letting the other police force know you are operating in their city, right?

Snelson: Definitely!

TCV: When working on investigations, are you in plain clothes?

Snelson: When I was with property, we were a little more dressed up because we were doing search warrants during those days. My days with Crimes Against Persons, we conducted interviews and need to look professional.

TCV: Did it appear that the Crimes Against Property was less volatile than Crimes Against Persons?

Snelson: I was only in each department for two days, so I really don't know. However, in one case that I worked on when in Crimes Against Property was a juvenile who had stolen a gun from a friend's brother's house, then tried to sell it to a firearms dealer. The dealer realized it was a stolen gun by the serial number and because he had sold it a year before to the victim. He bought the gun from the kid just to get it off the street and then called the police. We were able to ID him from a photo lineup by the

victim and the gun dealer. We served a search warrant on his house and plan to get the suspect's statement on what happened.

So, you can be dealing with situations where you go to a house on a search warrant and not know if there are more stolen guns around. It can be volatile in that respect. Of course, when dealing with crimes versus persons, the victim(s) and victim's family is just that much more irate because it involves an assault on a person.

TCV: When working with the Crimes Against Persons, what did you see?

Snelson: I worked with Detective [Jeremy] Miskella who handles sex registrants for Fremont. I was there when he registered a few "PC 290" (Penal Code 290 - Sex Offender Registration Act) registrants. That was an interesting process to see. I briefly helped him with the paperwork. The Department of Justice sends him a list of people who may have not registered. He does some background work to see if they have registered and may be stuck in the system or have not registered and need to be found. He was very tenacious about it and I think he is doing a great job.

I also worked with Detective [Mark] Dang who was getting a juvenile warrant signed from the stolen gun that I spoke about previously.

TCV: Did you see any overlap between Crimes Against Property and Crimes Against Persons?

Snelson: I didn't see a lot of overlap when I was there, but remember it was only a few days. There is probably overlap when we get big cases. I don't know how it is handled when that does happen.

TCV: What is the caseload like in these departments?

Snelson: It is hard for me to know since I was only working with these departments for a short time. I know there is quite a bit going on. There was an armed robbery when I was working with the Crimes Against Persons unit and Detective Dang took a part of that. We spent time on PC (Probable Cause) Declarations. The perpetrators were arrested on Thursday night and were going to be held over the weekend. The law says they have to see a judge within 48 hours or you have to have PC Declarations signed by a judge saying that the person or people can be held over the weekend and see the judge on Monday. That was a "spur of the moment thing" so since it happened on a Thursday night, Detective Dang needed to drop everything to get the declarations done on Friday.

I didn't get into the prioritizing of cases, but I saw stacks of folders with different pieces of work that needed to be done for investigations.

TCV: You are now back to patrol during the swing shift. Do you revisit investigations or was this experience designed to give you a quick look at another facet of the force?

Snelson: I think the idea is to give me a brief look at these departments. It is good that this is happening after I have been in training at the street level for a while. Now I understand how reports taken on the street are elevated to a

full-blown investigation by a detective. The better the work on the street, the better it is for the detective to be able to "pick up the ball and run." This helped me to get a bird's eye view and see how the system works.

TCV: Did this experience open your eyes to additional possibilities that you might pursue later in your career?

Snelson: It is a different pace. You are reading reports and meeting with other detectives to try to get your mind around a picture of what happened and seeing what can be done to prosecute those who have committed these crimes. You have a little more time to focus on cases. I am sure that I will want to spend some time in investigations during my career.

I was able to write a search warrant and an arrest warrant in the two days I spent with Crimes Against Property and that is invaluable experience. This is another tool in your toolbox as a Fremont Police officer and, as we have talked about previously, the training goal is to train officers who are not just "niche" officers, but have experience in a broad range of areas. I want to learn as much as possible in different areas.

TCV: How are you doing so far?

Snelson: It is going really well. Coming back on swing shift, we had a "in progress" burglary. Some guys had set off the internal motion detector at a stereo store and the alarm company had microphones in their system, so we were listening to the guys talking as they were robbing the place. We brought one guy from the south side, a K-9 unit first on scene from the north and my car came in third before we engaged the suspects. It was the first time that I have been involved in that type of situation. We are able to sneak up on the suspect outside loading the van. We went in along with the K-9. A suspect took some steps to flee and realized the K-9 was running at him and jumped into the van and to the roof, but his leg was dangling and the dog grabbed his leg and yanked him off. We cuffed the suspect and put him in another car that showed up.

We secured the perimeter of the location and Officer [Richard] Zemlok heard footsteps on the roof and "called it out." Sergeant [Patrick] Epps talked the guy off the roof. We yelled into the building that we were going to send a dog in at least six times, suspecting that there was at least one more suspect. We cut the lock to the rollup door and opened it and sent the dog in. Another suspect was found hiding behind a display model. It was a good experience. The group of officers did a great job communicating with each other and setting up a perimeter. Sergeant Epps was the commanding sergeant on scene. He let everyone know that, after securing the perimeter, time was on our side and we could wait for the proper time and equipment - CHP helicopter, etc. - to ensure safety.

TCV: The K-9 units are quite an asset.

Snelson: Huge! They are very smart and I am amazed at how controlled they are. Officer [Jason] Davison's dog, Kanto, obeys every command! A huge asset! These units are often used when there is a possibility of someone hiding or running. That night, about 1 a.m., we had a number of officers that could respond. In another recent situation, we had a call from someone saying that a man in the house had outstanding warrants. We did a check and one of them was for evading police. We know him as someone who runs. With a total of four officers - I am counted as one even though there are actually two of us, my Field Training Officer and myself - we went to the house and it would have been better with more officers since he saw us and fled before the K-9 arrived. That is a sign of the times - we don't have enough police officers on the street. We are currently operating at minimums because of budget constraints.

TCV: Are you still enjoying the training?

Snelson: Yes! I have learned that my FTO is always right. I will think that I have "this one figured out" and find out that I should do something else. I am currently with my second FTO, Officer [Kevin] Gott, a 20+ year veteran. If my FTO's are an example of all the trainers that Fremont has, we have some excellent trainers! It must be difficult for them since I am moving at 1 mile per hour when they are used to working at Mach 1! They are very patient.

Traffic and 'Mid' Shift

Officers Matthew Bocage, Ramin Mahboobi and Matthew Snelson are scheduled to complete supervised field training next month. Recently, they have been working with the Traffic Division and relate some of their experiences and thoughts at this point of training.

Bocage: We are just coming off our investigative traffic week and starting the midshift. The last few weeks have been pretty exciting. My FTO is Officer Javier Marquez; a very experienced officer. In the course of four days, we had about 28 moving violations. The approach to traffic is different than patrol. It took some adjustment.

Mahboobi: Traffic is involved with safety enforcement.

Bocage: Right! Traffic is focused on violations such as running red lights, speeding, seat belts, etc. I learned how to pace cars and that was interesting and exciting. No one is happy to be pulled over and get a ticket so everyone has a bit of an attitude, but it was interesting. I would say 75-80% of people denied the very thing I stopped them for. They absolutely denied it! People are funny that way.

TCV: Were there many incidents of extremely poor or dangerous driving?

Bocage: I would say the incidents I saw were within the norm. We were in a marked vehicle and most people were alerted to our presence.

Mahboobi: I wrote about 30 tickets. My FTO was Officer Dan Harvey who knows a lot about traffic enforcement and opened up the vehicle code to me; there is so much in the vehicle code. To answer your question, there were several times when I turned on my lights that drivers reacted in a strange manner. They didn't know what to do.

In one case, I activated my lights to stop a car and the driver slammed on its brakes and stopped in the lane. In another instance, as I was pulling a car over to the shoulder, another vehicle passed me on the right shoulder of the road! The people in the car looked back waving with anger!! The driver finally figured out that she was in the middle of a police stop and "floored it" out of there.

In another case, I was stopping another vehicle and a pickup truck traveling along the same street was approaching a signaled intersection. They froze when they saw me and decided to stop as the light was about to turn red but locked their brakes and skidded about 85 feet into the middle of the intersection.

What was interesting was that when people admitted that they had done something wrong and understood why, they were shocked that I wrote a ticket.

TCV: Did you notice that cell phones were a problem?

Bocage: A lot of people I stopped were on cell phones at the time. Our CHP collision forms have a box that you check that designates whether someone was talking on a cell phone at the time of the collision. It seems as if everyone is on a phone all the time.

Mahboobi: The state is keeping track of what was happening at the time of a collision - what actions might have distracted a driver prior to the accident. Sometimes I see a car swerving early in the day and wonder if we have a drunk driver that early. When I pull up, it may turn out to be someone who is lost, holding a cell phone and reading a map.

Bocage: I pulled a guy over who ran a stop sign and found that he had a map draped across the steering wheel. The driver claimed that the violation wasn't his fault because he was trying to read the map!

TCV: Was there anything about Traffic that was surprising?

Bocage: I enjoyed the opportunity to focus on traffic violations. It helped me to fine tune my ability to recognize violations. I feel very good about the mechanics of traffic stops.

Mahboobi: I was amazed at how busy that department is. I spent four long and busy days - I was exhausted at the end of each day. There were so many stops and contacts. People often are unhappy with the stop and feel they shouldn't be penalized for what others are also doing. They don't realize how many people the traffic officer deals with each day including serious traffic accidents. I am impressed with how much they do and how much is accomplished in one shift! We also responded to some calls to assist patrol - a bank robbery and a foot pursuit.

Bocage: I was impressed too! They are an extremely productive unit and I would love to work with the unit.

TCV: Are traffic units assigned to a specific area?

Mahboobi: No, complaints and concerns from citizens are used as a guide to where traffic patrols might locate. There are "hot spots" that are known for violations; detailed records are kept to find out where enforcement is needed.

Bocage: When traffic responds to citizen complaints and makes stops, especially in residential neighborhoods, people are happy to see action taken to protect them and their children.

TCV: Matt, you are on a different schedule, what are you doing now?

Snelson: I am on "Midnights" now. It is a bit different. Almost all calls are "in progress" or had just been "in progress." As an example, my first week on "mids," we had an auto burglary in progress when someone saw a burglar taking a stereo out of a car and reported it. We chased the suspect and recovered the stereo.

The pace is a bit different although I haven't worked a weekend shift yet, so there may be some big differences. It appears that Swing Shift is a much faster pace than "Midnight." Swing shift is on duty for about four hours before the midnight shift is on the street.

TCV: Since you have worked on different shifts and learned some techniques such as light management, do you find that some things are more familiar and a bit easier?

Snelson: I am finding more calls that are similar to what I have done before. It is still a mechanical process; I have to think through things and I am not moving as fast as I should. As an example, if I pull someone over and decide the car should be towed because someone is driving with a suspended license. There are a few things I need to do in that case. First, I need to write a citation for the driver, a CHP tow form, notify dispatch that I need a tow truck and dispatch needs vehicle information for records management. In one case, it was raining and I was trying to get the driver a taxi, so I was also working on that too! An experienced officer might take 30 minutes

to take care of everything and for me, it might take an hour. I need to tighten up on time management.

I was thinking about the importance of highly visible street numbers on houses. There have been many times that we are traveling down a street on a 911 call and people are depending on fast response; finding the house is difficult since the numbers are hidden or small. There is no consistency of where numbers are located either.

TCV: Any interesting experiences you can tell us about?

Snelson: I pulled over a guy who was driving with his lights out and it turned out that he was on parole. A search of his car turned up nothing of note. While I was handling the driver, my FTO was talking with a female passenger who, when asked for identification opened her purse and which contained a 14" knife in a sheath. She claimed the driver put it in her purse when they were being stopped. The driver had taken a little longer than normal to stop and that made me suspicious. He was cited for driving with lights off and the passenger for carrying the knife. The driver's parole officer was notified and will handle any parole violation issues.

Later, I thought about that knife and the fact that the driver could have decided to come at me with it. I appreciated all the things I was taught at the academy and by my FTO. You have to be consistent when stopping cars because you don't know if it's "mom" or a parolee. Some people at night will grimace when light is shined in the car, but the reality is that I don't know who they are and what I will be facing. I will be looking at someone's hands when approaching because your eyes are not going to hurt me, but your hands might. That has to be balanced with communicating with people.

TCV: As you near the evaluation period to complete the FTO training, are you confident of your abilities?

Snelson: Yes, I think you have to go into that with confidence. If you do this passively, you will not do the things you need to do. There is no other way to be a solo officer than to do it! I have four more weeks of midnight shift with my tertiary FTO and then two weeks with my primary FTO for evaluation. If I pass all that, I can be released as a solo officer. You can be extended to allow some extra time for training. That is very common.

TCV: Has the academy training receded into the background?

Mahboobi: I see the academy as the core of my training and the on-the-job experience is what I am working with every day and building on.

Bocage: When you get the academics and fundamentals at the academy, they are essential for the job. Now I have a chance to fine tune my technique and integrate my personality with the job.

Snelson: There are many things taught in academy for safety and academics that are a good foundation. But, now that we are on the street, there is a different level of knowledge that is based on our experiences. I am now operating more on a Fremont

Police Department training standpoint than I was when coming out of the academy.

TCV: How do you feel about your growth in this profession?

Snelson: I know the things I am doing wrong and put a lot of personal pressure on myself to excel and succeed. This is a self-driven job. When you go out on your own as an officer, you have a choice of what to do, so you have to be self-driven and self-critical. From what I have heard and seen, I think all of us are on track. We may be extended in our training, but that isn't a negative thing in our line of work.

A few FTO's have told me that I am too nice at times and I can see that. It is important to know when you need to be strong and in control without any appearance of weakness. I think I have kept my private life separate from work, although there are times when I have had an attitude at home, but I think that is more from the changing shifts and sleep cycles rather than who I am.

Bocage: My comfort level has increased a bit. My friends and family have commented that I look a little more relaxed.

Mahboobi: I see the confidence level increasing in all of us. You start to believe in yourself - that you can do this. In the beginning, it is so overwhelming. Looking back, as a person it changes you. I know that I have grown so much! I feel more confident each time I go out. I still know that I have so much more to learn. I have not found my comfort level on the job yet, but I do have confidence that I can do the job. I am now able to relax a little when off duty. My friends and family have seen that too.

Bocage: It is easy to lose perspective of what this is all about. We are constantly second-guessing and asking what I could do better, but that introspection is part of the process. I am okay with that now and understand that I have a lot to learn, but it can be done.

Snelson: I now have a great appreciation for the complexity that police officers face on every call. Before entering this profession, some things appear very straightforward and easy but from a police officer's perspective, there are many decisions and concerns that need to be addressed; Is the environment safe? What crime was committed? Investigation and evaluation concerns, time management and coverage issues. This is a very complex profession.

Finding Their Footing

Officers Matthew Bocage, Ramin Mahboobi and Matthew Snelson are currently working with their "Tertiary FTO" (third Field Training Officer) to complete formal training, working in tandem under direct supervision. Here are their thoughts as they work "Mids" (8 p.m. - 7 a.m.).

TCV: Now that you have been working the "Mid" Shift for a while, is there anything distinctive about policing that time period?

Mahboobi: Each shift is different from each other. The volume of calls waiting is very high from the beginning of Swing Shift; people are starting to come home from work and domestic activity increases. Mids can be that way, but sometimes things are quieter allowing proactive police work. After 3 a.m., the calls we get are primarily "in progress" when someone is awakened by an attempted burglary or theft. These are exciting to respond to since the crime is happening then.

Snelson: All shifts have their own pattern. The midnight shift tends to be action oriented calls. The day shift ends up getting a lot of "cold" reports where there is no suspect on scene, but the incident has just been discovered. Swing shift hits the ground running since kids are getting home from school, adults from work and everyone's home. Midnights are sporadic when some nights seem to hop requiring more

officers since they can be "in progress." Our numbers can be depleted quickly during these times.

TCV: Can you get to the scene while the perpetrator is still around?

Bocage: It depends. The likelihood of arriving when the suspect is still around is greater in Mids since there is little traffic at that time and we can be on scene within a very short period of time. In the day shift, we are often called when someone discovers a burglary but they only know it happened sometime during the day.

Mahboobi: During a day shift, sometimes we were able to set up a perimeter and catch the suspect, but often they had already left the area. During Mids, a high percentage of the time, we are on scene when the suspect is still there or in the area and can be apprehended. It is hard for a suspect to blend into the background late at night since most people are inside and asleep.

When we patrol during the early morning hours, we can observe others and ask ourselves, "Is this normal activity for someone at this hour?" We may investigate with a "consensual encounter" where we may ask if it is okay to talk with the person and find out what they are doing. Sometimes stopping someone for a minor infraction in those early hours can lead to significant law enforcement issues.

Bocage: During Mids, we have the opportunity, after things have settled down a bit between 3 a.m. and 7 a.m. to write reports - a big help for us [rookies]. We are still very active on patrol, but citizen calls for service slow down. The number of officers on the street at that time is limited - there are not enough of us - so if we have a call that requires assistance, we are stretched very thin for the rest of the city. There may not be any cover units available and that affects how we handle violations and crimes.

Snelson: Down times allow more proactivity on midnights. There are areas we know that have problems and when we have time, observe and take action, if possible. There tend to be more criminals in ratio to other citizens late at night. I run across more parolees and those on probation on midnight shift.

TCV: **Do you find that with all the changes in shifts and now working during the night, your energy level goes through some radical changes?**

Bocage: I definitely go through ups and downs. I find that by the third or fourth day of the shift, I am running on fumes. I am constantly playing catch-up with my sleep patterns. On "off" days, I may sleep as much as 12 or 13 hours straight. It is tough, but it hasn't been that bad because this has

just been a few months. When we get through this period, things will stabilize.

TCV: **What is the difference between weekdays and weekends on the Mid Shift?**

Bocage: A huge difference! It will be very busy during a weekend.

Mahboobi: We may do bar checks of an area. We find out which bars have large crowds and have the greatest potential of problems. Later that evening, we pay close attention to those places. There is a big difference between weeknights and weekend nights.

TCV: **With the holidays approaching, are there more incidents of DUI (Driving Under the Influence)?**

Bocage: We have had our share of DUIs. In these few weeks, we have each had two or three that we have followed all the way through.

Snelson: I see a lot more DUIs at night. I have at least five DUIs now, all in the timeframe after midnight. One of the bars in my area has been having a lot of problems. Our sergeant may ask us to be nearby at closing time to prevent any fights from escalating.

Mahboobi: I feel there have been an abnormally high number of DUIs in the past few weeks. I have seen and taken reports on several DUI crashes where we investigate an accident and see that alcohol or drugs were involved. The report changes from an accident report to an extended report or reports. There is a lot of documentation - the traffic collision, what caused the collision, witnesses, involved parties, intoxication report, breath or blood test, etc. The amount of paperwork involved is amazing.

Bocage: Obviously, it is much better to catch these people prior to this happening.

Mahboobi: An increase in these types of statistics leads to heavier enforcement. As the holidays approach, people will be getting together to celebrate and the amount of DUI will increase. We are trying through heavy enforcement to prevent people from trying to drive home on their own while intoxicated. If they choose to do this, we hope to stop them before a collision occurs.

TCV: How do you handle someone who is intoxicated, but on foot?

Bocage: We try to apply the spirit of the law. If they are too intoxicated and cannot take care of themselves, they will be arrested. If a friend can help them get home, we advise them to go home directly. If the person is mildly intoxicated, but lucid, and on their way home - not a danger to themselves or anyone else - we let them go home.

If there is a problem with a particular bar, we will try to work with the bartenders and owners to let them know that they need to be aware of the age of their patrons and the potential for problems. Sometimes we will walk through and, if people appear underage, ask for identification.

Mahboobi: We are not trying to tell people how to run their businesses. Our business is to inform them of the law and work with them to stop illegal activity.

TCV: What happens when there is negative news about the use of Tasers or other police procedures?

Bocage: We definitely hear about these things. The department treats these things as an educational experience and as long as we are acting within our policies, we continue accepted methods of law enforcement. We do talk about these things at briefings.

Mahboobi: The Lieutenant will talk about something that may have happened within our own department, neighboring agencies or elsewhere. We try not to second-guess another officer's judgment but try to discuss the facts and actions that led to the incident. All the facts and factors may not be known, so we try to learn from what we do know. The department spent a long time developing policies for the Taser and every officer that has one has spent a long training day on the use of them.

Briefings will cover what has happened in our area, around the Bay Area and beyond - information that will help us during our shift. If we need to be on the lookout for particular suspects or vehicles, that will be covered. Radio and dispatch personnel may come and awards are given at briefings.

Bocage: I feel very informed coming out of briefing.

TCV: At this point, if you were told that FTO training had ended and you were to patrol on your own without accompaniment by another officer, could you do it?

Bocage: I am comfortable enough to be able to do it. I am not sure that I am ready, but I have enough tools to learn on the fly. A couple of months ago, I would have been very uneasy about it. You are never out there alone since there are cover officers and support from the department.Right now, my FTO, Tony Tassano, stays in the background as an observer on calls, but we are constantly discussing procedures afterwards.

I am really going to appreciate being "10-8," on my own. When I am working with these people and engage as a patrol officer, I will have come full circle. No longer will I be filling in all the blanks, it becomes a team effort rather than someone holding back and evaluating how I am doing. We have averaged about one arrest per shift which is above average. I know that some of those have been due to my observations and diligence.

Mahboobi: I am confident that I would be able to do it. There is still a lot that we don't know, but you never will know it all and there is some that we will not know until we do it. If they cut me loose right now, I know a lot about officer safety and would not put myself in danger. I am more oriented with the city streets and can get to a "hot" situation. I know how to start off calls and can find help to reach a final disposition, if necessary. If an unclear situation occurs, I know how to find help through resources available to me. That is something I did not have earlier in the training.

My FTO, Gregory Pipp, doesn't say a word in most instances - he is observing. On scene, he steps back and lets me do what I have to do. My goal is to not turn to him at any time during the call. We discuss my procedures after the call.

When we are cut loose, in real life, there is a team effort to take care of a situation. Right now, everyone is standing back to see what I can do and waiting for direction from me. That is good because it makes me think of everything that needs to be done.

Snelson: About a week and a half ago, my FTO, Officer [Joseph] Geibig, asked me to drive my own car. He rode with me the first week and in the second week, I began driving my own vehicle. On my "Friday" of my second week with Officer Geibig, at the beginning of the shift, he directed me to get my own car. That was a great moment! Within three minutes on the street, I made a traffic stop. I have probably made over a hundred traffic stops with an FTO, but walking to the car that time, I was so amped up, so excited internally. I had to tell myself to relax and breathe. Within a few hours of being on my own, I started to get that under control. It was definitely a different feeling - there isn't someone in the car evaluating every move you make.

I think I made the transition to being capable of working solo in phase two when I was working with Officer [Kevin] Gott, the expectation was "OK kid, show me what you can do!" He wanted to step back and watch me do it. I don't believe there was a single day when I made the transition but I felt I was moving towards this goal.

Officer Geibig drives a second car and "shadows" although he doesn't drive right behind me. I am doing my own policing. After a big call, he and I will discuss my actions. Recently, on a burglary call, I was the primary officer and he and I met afterwards to critique my performance. We still show up as one unit on the roster and are viewed as one unit on the street. Dispatch will not dispatch us separately even though Officer Geibig may not be needed on the call.

I have found that when working on a big call, the team effort comes through not only during the call, but when handling the paperwork. Other officers will ask if they are needed to write a supplemental report to augment the primary officer's "umbrella" report. A cover officer working with me is no longer evaluating my performance; rather we are working as part of a team effort.

On a call, I can now make sure I know exactly where the location is, while with an FTO in the car, you don't want to be looking something up all the time. You want to look like you know exactly what you are doing and where you are going. If I have to stop at the curb for five seconds to confirm where I am going, it's better because when I move, I can concentrate on driving, what type of call I am responding to and what I need to do when I get there.

It definitely is "freeing." We couldn't have done this until now because we didn't have the tools. Being solo now, a lot of the training is coming home. I feel that I have a lot to prove. You don't want to be known as a slacker. I want to be known as working for the team and effective for the City of Fremont.

Out of the Nest, Ready to Fly

F remont rookie police officers Matthew Bocage, Ramin Mahboobi and Matthew Snelson are entering the final phase of the Field Training Officer (FTO) program designed to provide on-the-job training under the guidance of experienced police officers. Each rookie has now had some experience operating as a solo officer and will return to their initial FTO for final evaluation and approval prior to field assignment.

TCV: What is happening now?

Mahboobi: I am now on "shadow" and will go back to my original FTO, Officer Jim Koeph. This is the check-out phase. Many weeks have passed from the time I originally worked with him so he will now evaluate me to see where I have progressed and where there are concerns, if any. He will address those and then back off into a complete shadow phase where I am in a vehicle, on my own, logging on as a sole police officer. My FTO will monitor me over the airwaves and show up at some of the scenes to observe how I operate. The goal for him is to "not exist" but just watch. This is a test of whether I can do this job on my own and function as a solo occupant of the vehicle.

Bocage: What I think they like to try to do is break you into the "shadow" phase before it actually starts with your primary FTO. My FTO, Officer Tony Tassano, wore plain clothes this last week. People are looking at me rather than him. I got the majority of attention on calls. This is how they step things up a bit - let the leash go, so to speak.

On Friday, I was with another FTO, Officer Steve Solaro who was told by Officer Tassano that I was ready to experience a solo patrol and I did. My call sign went out with my name. It was very exciting; very, very different! Little things like having the passenger seat for my gear was neat since with another officer, you have to jump out and retrieve things from the trunk. Just pulling out of the gate with no one else in the car was exhilarating!

When we are in "shadow" phase, the FTO dresses in uniform but has a different car. Their call sign is their badge number and they will monitor your calls. Occasionally they will show up on your calls, sometimes when you do, sometimes halfway through or at the end of the call or, they may not show up at all. The FTO is "invisible" for the most part and does not show up as a separate patrol. If I need a cover officer, another officer - a zone partner - will show up.

Snelson: Last week was the last week in my third phase. My tertiary FTO, Officer [Joseph] Geibig was on vacation, so I spent the first few days with Officer John Anderson in the car with me since he doesn't know me and needed to make sure that I am safe to be out and about. The last two days I drove on my own and he "shadowed" me. I have been struck by the amount of wisdom out there with these veteran officers. This week I went back to my primary FTO, Officer [Norberto]Quimson on Days. I will be finishing with him - he is doing the final evaluation. He rode with me for a couple of days in plain clothes and then the plan is for him to shadow.

Each time you meet a new FTO, it takes a bit of time to get to know each other. It doesn't really throw you since we have been doing this for so long, but it is an adjustment. They are trying to find your strengths and weaknesses and you are trying to in this last phase, since I have worked previously with Officer Quimson, I understood more easily what he is looking for and expects.

TCV: Have you been driving as a solo officer?

Mahboobi: Yes, with my third FTO, Officer Greg Pipp, over the last week. We did a shift when he wore civilian clothes to look like a ride-along so none of the people involved would turn to him. This was to determine if I could handle things on my own but with his presence just in case he needs to step in.

I had a really good shift, felt comfortable with him there being able to handle things as if he wasn't there. I was able to make decisions. I feel that I can handle most of the calls I am going to now, doing the things I need to do and am becoming a little bit more fluid.

I know that I often have the discretion to do one of a couple of things and my decision will be right and "in policy," but I still need more experience to be sure that I am doing the right thing for the person involved. Could I go with Plan B? In the past, I get to that point and run it by my FTO telling him what I am going to do and if he doesn't have anything else to say, that is the way I will go.

In the past, I have used my FTO as a "safety net." This week I have not done that at all. Even if I get to that point, I think it through myself and decide how I am going to "close it" and without looking at my FTO, finish the contact with the person. When we get back in the car leaving the scene, I tell my FTO what I did and why. He will either say, "Okay, that's fine" or "Do you realize what else you could have done?" I will respond with the choices I had and why I made my decision. He is usually happy with that since I am seeing the overall picture.

After the shift where my FTO was in civilian clothes, we went to Shadow Phase which was outstanding! I got into my vehicle and left the parking lot without my FTO. It was an adrenaline rush that is hard to describe! 'I am really on my own and this is my first night as me.'

Everything will be done as I want to do it. Everything will finish with my final answer with no outside influence. For a second, I thought 'Holy Cow, this is overwhelming.' But, I went out there and the great thing was that I felt very comfortable. I knew that I wasn't going to get myself in trouble and was confident that I would not do anything dumb.

Officer Pitt really opened it up for me. In this phase alone, I felt a big transition. In the last two weeks he opened up my vision to what I am seeing at night - how to foresee things and understand what is coming at me rather than react to what already happened. That made a big difference when I was on my own. I didn't have to call him once. He assured me that if I called him he would be right there - that I wouldn't be on my own. I handled my calls in a reasonable amount of time with the correct conclusion. I made several proactive traffic stops, wrote a few tickets and gave a few warnings. I was real confident of what I was doing. That was a real difference of not having the FTO next to you making you nervous. You don't have the pressure of someone sitting next to you.

I have had great FTOs but there is a pressure of their presence which makes me second-guess my actions. Being solo, things are clear as a bell without the pressure of scrutiny of every single thing I do. I was able to get to where I needed to go. In a few instances, I was unfamiliar with where I was supposed to go but it was no problem - I take my book, my resources and quickly know exactly where to go. In the same instance with my FTO, I would get nervous about whether I am going to get marked down for that. It was like a whole new job. It was the best week I have worked in this career!

Bocage: There is a difference in how backup officers treat you now. The training wheels are off now. Everyone knows that you are fresh into it and helps. Ramin [Mahboobi] and I were going solo on the same day (in different zones) and I was constantly monitoring his calls; we were both being as proactive as we could, volunteering for assignments.

Snelson: What I have realized after driving on my own is that the calls I felt were basic became a bit more ambiguous since now there is no "safety blanket" of an FTO by my side. I need to figure out the process and dealing with the issue. It is a healthy transition; now if there is a question, I ask my cover officers. There is wisdom and experience on almost every call I go to from other officers. When I have a question, I can look to someone else, but now they are my partner in this rather than an FTO.

TCV: Was this a quantum leap for you?

Bocage: A total quantum leap. It is like night and day. You are free to do what you want and no one is evaluating every little move that you make. If you take the long way to a call or get a bit lost, there is no one to see that. You can make little mistakes and learn from them without the pressure of someone watching. By the same token, you are absolutely responsible for your safety - there is no one to correct you in the middle of something. You have complete ownership of who you are, what you do, what you represent and your own personal safety. I feel pretty good about things. I still have a lot of questions, but there are others to help if you need it - cover officers and supervisors.

Mahboobi: I wouldn't have been comfortable six weeks ago. I wouldn't have had the confidence to make investigative stops. There were calls during this shadow phase that I took without hesitation. I know that even if I struggle with something, I will come out with the right answer. I need more experience and training; every shift I work will be another day I learn something. I believe in myself and have confidence to say that one way or another I will get the information to solve a problem. If I get jammed up, I know where the resources are to get the answer.

It's all about repetition and training. Every call is unique, but now we have seen enough to know how to handle the situation. The way you solve problems is pretty consistent. Once you understand your resources, you know where to go to help with each situation.

Snelson: I think I can go out and handle in a rough way most calls that come my way. Over the years I will become more finely tuned and smoothed out. I have appreciated and seen cover officers, after a call, pull me aside and help me refine my

techniques. I can see that process going on for many years. Many senior officers tell me that even now they confer with other officers to discuss what they are seeing in a situation. It is a foolish person who thinks they have everything worked out.

I feel confident that I can go out and do these things. It feels good to be at this point. I look forward to the other end of five years from now and I can look back and say that I have handled quite a few things and feel confident that I can go to a majority of calls and handle them smoothly. I feel competent to do the job. I know that I will stay safe, I know I will protect the officers I am out with and I know that I will protect the public. That is the most important part. I feel I am at a safety level and competency level where I can go out on my own although you are never really on your own since you have partners and a sergeant to help.

TCV: Are you surprised that all of you have been successful so far during your training?

Mahboobi: Not at all. I had no doubt about our abilities to do it. I thought "we will get through this" when we first started. In the beginning when we got hit with all the information to absorb, it was overwhelming. I began to question whether I could handle all the complexities of the job. As we worked through it and I could see the progression of Matt Bocage who was working the same shifts and compare how we were doing. We would hear about Matt Snelson and knew he was doing well. We worked together at the academy so we were able to watch and help each other. I hear that the others are doing okay and that I am doing okay too. We have become very good friends and see each other off duty.

Bocage: It was very helpful to have others going through the same experience with me. Our lockers are right next to each other. At the end of a shift, Ramin and I were able to compare notes and lean on each other. Matt [Snelson] was on a different shift, so we didn't get to see him as much but the three of us were able to relate our frustrations, experiences, excitement and growth was great. It is probably tougher to do on your own.

TCV: There will be a new group of rookies entering the FTO program about the time the three of you leave it. How will you respond to them?

Mahboobi: We owe it to them to sit down and give them the benefit of our experiences. In a way, we were able to get the same information from others in the department who had finished academy and the FTO program most recently. They were able to talk about the academy and what to expect as well as insights into the FTO program. It was helpful to hear them and understand what to expect. We knew that we could contact them if we had questions. We were assigned mentors - veteran officers - that gave us information about the FTO program. Others officers offered advice and anecdotes that helped us see some humor in our situation. It lightened the atmosphere for us. It would be real selfish of us if we didn't turn around and give information and guidance to those who are following us. Each of us

has contacted the new hires and told them to contact us at any time if they need to talk.

Bocage: We will be able to relate well to them since we will have just completed our FTO training. More than likely, I will work with or come in contact with one of them since there are five of them and they will rotate through different shifts. I will give them whatever advice I can and some pointers.

Snelson: Being new officers in general, there is some camaraderie with other new officers. Being just six months out of the [academy] process, I may have more empathy for them than some others. They have been at academy for six weeks and only spent a few weeks in Fremont before leaving so we didn't have a chance to get to know them well before they left for academy. I spoke with one of them today and I remember my feelings when I was close to finishing the academy - how they are still getting a lot of pressure from Training Officers at the academy. We talked about getting together after they get out of the academy and sitting down with the three of us that will have just finished FTO and the five of them that will be entering the program. We might have some insight on how to prepare mentally for the FTO program. It is always easier to go into a process with some knowledge about what it is like.

On my midnight shift, Officers Jacob Shannon and Armando Magana were both the last recruits that went through academy before us. They are just clearing probation (one year) now. Officer Shannon was saying that it is nice to see newer officers on the street. We talked about going through probation, going solo, what to expect. It's a cycle! There are already guys in academy behind those who will soon be graduating. My sense is that it takes a good three to five years of police work on a daily basis until you get to the point where things click as second nature.

I am still a rookie. Obviously there is a maturation process and these officers have "shed some weight" clearing probation becoming full-fledged members of the department. There is a change, but not a feeling of knowing it all. When I look at the senior members of our department who I believe are really good officers, these are people who don't stop learning. One officer spoke about the Miranda Law (citizen rights when arrested) which has changed three times since he has been a police officer. Just because you learn something one way in academy doesn't mean that it will always remain the same way. Things always change; you have to be adaptable and flexible.

TCV: Now that you have been on your own, will you feel more comfortable when you ride with your primary FTO in the shadowing phase?

Mahboobi: Now that I have worked as a solo officer, I will feel more confident. I have shown myself that I can go out there and do what I need to do. There may be suggestions of better ways to do things, but I am confident that I will do things correctly. In the past, the presence of my FTO made me second-guess. Now I know that I don't

need to do that because I have proven my ability to myself. I anticipate some uncomfortable feelings but I am going to do things just as if I was solo. Having experienced a solo patrol, I know what it is like.

TCV: Would you change anything in the training regimen?

Snelson: Honestly, I cannot think of too many things I would tweak. I liked "Midnights" since they have a lot of hot calls. Things are happening quickly and you need to put all the pieces together rapidly. I can't say that I would want to give up any time on "Swing" or "Day," but another shift of "Mids" would have been just that many more experiences of those calls. At the same time, I feel that I am ready to make the transition to a solo officer and would not want to extend another week. I do know that through the process, I feel prepared. I was thinking of how to encapsulate the process philosophically and looking at it, the youngest FTO that I have had has been on for about eleven years. That is a long time as a police officer - some have been on over twenty. It is a process of passing on learned wisdom and knowledge from the veteran officers to the rookie officer. That is the point. To pass that on so you can become a proficient, competent officer more quickly. If I look at it in that light, the process has done very well.

Mahboobi: I think it is pretty much on track. If I didn't feel as confident as I do now, having gone through some shadow phase, I would say another week or two with the FTO in the car. The program has already been extended to 18 weeks, so we have spent a lot of time experiencing as many calls as we can. The amount of time in each phase was appropriate. For instance the week in Traffic taught us a lot about the vehicle code and how to be objective and focus on safety rather than just on every little violation. It taught us how to be fair. The week in Investigation was excellent - what type of cases get to them and how they are handled - and how to use that resource and be of assistance to that department. I wouldn't want to extend the program, but I think it is necessary time in training. It is well thought out. Looking back, I can't say that I would change anything.

Bocage: I think they have it pretty well dialed in. It was challenging at times, but necessarily so. I felt a little overwhelmed by paperwork at times, but the goal is to get you as much exposure as they can. That is what we were told from the very beginning. Looking back, you get a little frustrated and overwhelmed but it was necessary. I have a wide range of experiences, being able to take primary on many things in the zone. You are buried in paperwork but it is an invaluable experience. I have an idea of how to handle a lot of different types of calls. I think they have done a great job with the Fremont program. We haven't spoken much about the academics, but we are taking tests all the time - I will be taking my final next week - we have binders full of information. It is a well-oiled machine. Much depends on your FTO, but we have good, solid people here. It's excellent.

This week, I am going through another big change in my life. Tomorrow I am proposing to my long-time girlfriend, Raquel Leon. Raquel is a teacher at Alvarado Middle School, Union City.

Call Signs

All three rookies have now successfully completed FTO training and will operate as solo officers during the remainder of their probationary period that will end December 2005. Another interview is planned in about six months after time spent as "10-8" solo officers.

TCV: Each of you has now completed the final two weeks of the FTO program. Was it a tough two weeks?

Snelson: It was nerve-wracking to some degree. You are trying to put everything together and do things well; to give confidence to your primary FTO. You want to come back and show that you really know what you are doing; that you are competent. You don't want to make mistakes. I think that at this point we know what we should be doing and now it is just putting it all together.

It was kind of cool to come back to the same group that saw me when I started - the early day shift on "A" side. I am sure I looked like the scared little rookie the first few weeks. Coming back, getting razzed a little bit, joking around and going out and getting business done. It was fun to come back and feel like a competent member of the team.

Mahboobi: I echo much of what Snelson just said. What made it nerve-wracking was that this was the shift that saw you at your "vulnerable" time. Now you are supposedly trained and you want to come back and show them what you have learned. The other thing that adds to this is that I am coming from being a solo vehicle in the third phase and then back to having a training officer in the car again. During the first couple of days, I wanted to show my primary FTO that I know what I am doing.

Once the work week got started, time just flew by. We were so busy that I didn't think about the training program because once my FTO spent two shifts with me to see what had been delivered back to him, I was solo for the rest of that week and the last week. There were days that I didn't see him except at briefings and at the end of the day. I was extremely busy in the last week and because of that, I almost forgot I was in "Shadow" phase. It was as if that was already done; everyone around me was treating me as if I was past the FTO training. We are just getting the job done.

It is amazing to see a different side of it since when you are in the FTO program, everyone steps back and makes you work your way through all phases of the entire scene. Now you see the other side where everyone just jumps in to get the job done.

Bocage: My Shadow phase was a bit different since it was split in half - half on mid-shift with Officer Tony Tassano and half on day shift with my primary who had been on vacation, Officer Gregg Crandall. Initially there is a lot of anxiety. I am driving around and calling out every single street that I get on - just talking to myself. I am saying this so just in case I go on the air, I know my location. Once you get into it things are okay.

My FTOs gave me a lot of confidence. They cut the leash. They said, "Maybe I will show up and maybe I won't." I didn't even feel like I was in training anymore because like Ramin said, when you show up on these calls, no one is looking at you to handle everything from start to finish anymore. It is more of a collaborative effort. You are working as a team. You just have to be sure that you are not a cog that is going to collapse the machine.

I had a fantastic two weeks - everyone was great. We started getting congratulatory emails and comments before we were done and I thought, 'Look, no one has shook my hand yet - we are not through - there are 36 hours left!' I think all of us had a good time. You just hope that nothing really explodes and you are presented with a situation that you are not sure how to handle. You want things to be within your level of competency and for me that is how it went down.

TCV: What happens when you finish the FTO program?

Snelson: On my last day, it was a normal day of patrol. I was out on my own and my FTO was writing my final evaluation. This is a packet that summarizes where you are as an officer and their recommendation for you. On that last day, Officer [Norberto] Quimson finally allowed me to take him out to lunch as a traditional thank you for his efforts.

In the morning he started going through his evaluation with me on some "down time," letting me know about my strengths and weaknesses and some classes he recommended for me in the future. Some that he recommended were interrogation classes, drug enforcement classes, evaluation classes - basically deepening my understanding. We talked a lot about that. Then I signed off on the written evaluation - signing on each page. This was pretty much like we have done every day through FTO on our evaluations.

There was also a sergeant evaluation that I also signed off. He then presented his final evaluation to the sergeant who then presented it to the lieutenant - it went up the chain of command that way. In the end, I believe it is the captain who makes the decision of whether we go "10-8" out on our own.

Mahboobi: My last day was very different because I had a heavy caseload coming into that day. I was under a lot of stress - I had one pretty high profile case of child molestation that I was trying to hammer through. It could have gone to the detectives but I wanted to keep it and my sergeant said that I could have the time necessary to work on it for the experience. This is one where I showed up solo and talked with the victim. I thought that 'they really must trust me if they are letting me handle it.' Coming into my last day, I had that case which had taken a lot of time over the last two days. I had three or four other cases too where I knew that through investigation I could get an arrest. I knew that these cases were good to have because that if I did the job right, we could put bad people in jail.

Any time I would go "10-8" in service for regular calls, I would end up at a cluster from another case that would take a side track to another investigation. By the time my "Friday" came up, I looked at my primary FTO and told him how busy I was and said that whatever we have to do, let's get it done. He had the same feeling. So he said we would meet throughout the day and have talks about the next phase.

I had no doubt that at the end of the shift I would make it through the program. I felt that for the entire week so there were no secrets about giving the blessing. My primary FTO, Jim Koepf, is a guy unbelievably filled with knowledge; I don't think there is a single directive or policy or law in the world that he doesn't know. He said, 'Its not just about getting out of FTO, you still have another year of probation. The FTO program is about getting you

to be a competent officer who continues and makes it through the probationary period without a hitch. The real goal is to get you through probation.' He reminded me that if I ever get jammed up, there is always help available. If you find yourself in a situation where you are unsure of what to do, you have to know who to contact and what resources you have.

We met several times during the day and he gave me advice about what to do from this point. He congratulated me and told me that it [finishing FTO] was a big accomplishment but it doesn't mean it is over. Don't ever stop learning. We had a really good talk but it was unfortunate that it was broken up during the day between trying to handle all these different cases and running around town. I read a final evaluation, signed off on it and my sergeant also presented me with a final evaluation that I read and signed off. There were handshakes and congratulations - it was a great feeling.

Bocage: I think my experience was a combination of the others. I didn't have nearly the caseload that Ramin had but I did have a few things I was working on this week. My primary FTO, Gregg Crandall and I put the finishing touches on the rookie book. We all take a written final in the last week or two.

TCV: Are the academics more practically oriented or do they center on rules and regulations?

Bocage: I would say they are more practically oriented. They are shaped around how the Fremont Police Department does things. A lot of it is directive driven. They want you to be competent in California procedures but finely honed in how Fremont does business.

TCV: Is there much about specific regulations.

Bocage: There is a lot of that and also scenario questions.

The orders of our permanent assignments were handed down via email throughout the department on our Tuesday. We knew they were pretty anxious to get us out there.

Mahboobi: It was interesting because we still had two days to go and an email goes out saying, 'The following recruits have successfully passed the FTO program' and gave us orders to take two days off and then return to our permanent assignment. Bocage and I looked at each other and said, 'I guess we are golden, what do you think?' My FTO looked at it and said, 'Now I feel like a lame duck!'

Bocage: We were assigned our permanent call signs, so I am now "2Xray2." I am staying in the same place I am now. I will be under my primary FTO on day shift, on "B" side for the next six months. So there wasn't a dramatic ending of my relationship with Officer Crandall. We are going to be in the same zone, working together on the same cases. That is very exciting for me.

Mahboobi: My call sign is 2Ocean11. I will be on the "A" side where Matt [Snelson] was working. I will be leaving the entire team I was working with so it is a bit sad. It is

going to be interesting; I will be working with officers that I haven't worked with yet. It will be a drastic shift. I don't doubt for a minute that it will be just as welcoming as on the "B" side.

I have heard nothing but good things about the personnel on that side. Matt has been on that side and all we have heard through the interviews is how helpful everyone has been. I am looking forward to the change, but it is also sad since I just got used to working with the "B" team knowing each person's style. However, I do get to meet more people throughout the department. I have always said that I am not concerned with what shift I get or who I work with; I am just happy to be here! I will be on swing shift.

Snelson: I am on the midnight shift. My official call sign is "1Adam10." I have been working a lot of Zone 3 because the shift that I am on is light on south Fremont units, so I have actually been working as "3-A-2" for the last few days. Same as Ramin, I did my training on "A" side so I have built a lot of relationships there. Going to "B" I don't know anyone at all, so there is some apprehension.

It is a great thing, however, to meet the other half of the department. So, while I was somewhat disappointed that I didn't continue the relationships that I started on the "A" side, now I have an opportunity to build relationships on the "B" side. Some of the FTO's that trained Matt and Ramin are on my shift and almost everyone has come up, given me their phone number and let me know they are available if I need anything. They are extremely helpful. I have not had any feeling of 'Okay rookie, you're here now, pull your weight.' It's a feeling of 'We are all here together; It's a team effort.' That is an awesome feeling. You get this impression that 'We have confidence in you, let's get it done. Now you are one of us.'

TCV: What will your relationship be with the rookies just entering the FTO program?

Mahboobi: We met with them just after our graduation from Sacramento academy and spent one week training together with the new rookies on their way to their academy giving them the benefit of our experiences. We are looking forward to help the guys who are just about to enter the FTO program.

Bocage: At the department Christmas party, we had the opportunity to see the junior officers there with their wives and girlfriends.

Snelson: Some of us had to work!

Bocage: We had a chance to talk with them. They were asking a lot of questions already. It will be neat to share our experiences with them. I know some of them will be coming to our shift and seeing some of the same FTOs we did.

TCV: Do you have any part in their training?

Snelson: On an emotional and experience level, we are closer to where they are, so we can probably relate to some of the things they are going through, but as far as educating them

to how to be a police officer, we are still trying to figure things out for ourselves. We still need to think through everything we do in the car and at some point with veteran officers, they reach a point where they can do things because they "feel" correct. I still feel very mechanical in my thought processes.

I think we may try to get together with them over the holidays where we can talk and joke about what it was like at the academy and then share some of our experiences in the FTO program.

Mahboobi: The new officers just graduated, so we would like to get together to congratulate them.

TCV: Ramin had a heavy caseload during his last few weeks. How was your last week during "shadow" phase? Any big cases?

Bocage: My week was routine but I am still learning and trying to absorb as much as possible from each call.

Snelson: Last week I had a big burglary case. By the time we were on scene, the suspects had left but they were stopped a few blocks away. One gave a confession. There was a lot going on - a few warrants I was allowed to write. One of the property detectives, [Paul] McCormick came out and on scene while we were investigating and offered a lot of help.

Officer [Donald] Martinez stopped a suspect - made a great stop - and did an amazing job of interrogating the suspect to the point where the person tells everything that happened. I have seen Officer Martinez do this twice and I don't think that would have happened if I had been the interrogating officer. It's a pleasure to see that work. I was on the other side with Officer Quimson and Sergeant [Robert] Lanci and Lieutenant [David] Lanier was back and forth between the two suspects. Seeing that whole scene - it was very intricate, very involved - trying to get things processed, getting fingerprints with a CSI [Crime Scene Investigator] trying to pull really good prints. That was a pretty involved case that took me all week.

What ends up happening when you get a big case is that you cannot just drop your zone partners - hide off the map in a corner somewhere. There are still cases and calls going on that generate reports. Some of them are not 'in progress' and can be held off for a bit, but at the same time you need to be diligent with those cases as well. The pressure builds up. I felt that but was able to deal with some of that on my first two days on my own. I think that is a constant process.

TCV: **Speaking of paperwork, do you feel that you are getting a handle on it?**

Bocage: Time management is the most critical thing. You have cases that can wait a little bit and then high priority cases. I am absorbing things better and definitely balancing things better but it is still a challenge for me. It is definitely something I have to get better at just so I don't feel this overbearing weight on my shoulders every time I go out there. It's a great feeling to be completely in the clear; when everything is taken care of.

Mahboobi: Just this last week, there was a residential burglary that was interrupted by the victim coming home. The suspect just walked right out of the front door, made some comments and left. The victim was able to give a pretty good description. We put out a vehicle description and a lot of good teamwork was in play right off the bat. A suspicious vehicle report had been taken earlier in the day by Officer Ken Lawrence. When he heard the 'in progress' report, Officer Lawrence jumped on the air and said that it sounded like his suspects from his case. He had a plate number whereas in my case, there was no plate number.

The teamwork was amazing. The crime analysis group was working up everything they could - any associated persons, etc. The channels were just flying. I am on the scene and there was a lot of evidence to be collected. I requested a CSI. My goal was to get this suspect. Time goes on; we got a photo of the primary suspect and we were trying to locate the suspect. The same day, I contacted detectives to ask what they knew about this person. They began to stake out houses to see if they can locate the suspect. The next morning the detectives were all over the Bay Area looking for the suspect. We were unable to locate the suspect. We didn't have a good address. I was trying to keep things a little bit clear that afternoon so if we did get an address, I would be free to write a warrant.

An hour later, I am working on the child molestation case and now I have that running too. On top of that, I had several other cases that also required investigation. I would go back and honor my zone responsibilities too. It seemed like every call I got to was something I could pick up and run with. I began to feel a lot of stress. I knew I could not handle everything at once. Currently, I am hammering them out. I went to my sergeant and told him of all the things that were going on and I was being buried in paperwork. He authorized some time off the street.

I spent my Friday from 6 a.m. - noon in the department to hammer out cases, trying to catch up. In that time, I took my final exam for the FTO program. I wasn't able to study for it since I had all these cases going on. My FTO wanted to review a bit before the exam, but we never got a chance to do it. This was my last day on FTO, unless I blew it having all these cases. I took the exam and passed it. I figured that I must know this stuff since I passed it. I got back out on the street and was dispatched to a hit-and-run with suspect information. The second I showed up there, there is call of a fight in progress. I had just made contact with the victim of the hit-and-run and I have a suspect but I have to go because I have a kid bleeding in the middle of the street somewhere. I gotta go so I told the victim that we would get another unit to them as soon as possible. We had a property crime and a crime against a person, so we have to respond to a threat of someone's life.

Now I end up with two juveniles arrested and booked, waiting for the parents. The whole time I am thinking that I will never get to finish my other cases. This took me until 4:30 p.m. and at 5 p.m. I am off duty, so I sat down at that point - it was my Friday and the last day of FTO - I finished my final evaluations and the formalities of the FTO program. Then I sat down to finish up the other cases since I couldn't put them on hold until I came back on duty. I finished about 12:30 a.m. I am off for today and then start my new shift tomorrow on swing shift. Hopefully, I will relax sometime. So, time management is the most important thing. I am learning a big lesson in time management right now.

TCV: What happens to the cases that you are currently working on now that some of you are being assigned to another shift?

Snelson: You keep running with them. I have a reported grand theft case. There were eight people reported to be in the house at the time of the theft. I have to interview all eight people for the case. Then I got the burglary case that I am wrapped up with too. Now I am going to midnight shift and who is up at 3 a.m. for an interview? Although this case was cleared up, I would probably have talked to a sergeant and asked for overtime to interview during the day. I would have worked my shift from 8 p.m. to 7 a.m. and then set up interviews for daytime and hammer them out. What you take, you finish. Part of the gratification of the job is to take these things to conclusion and bring them to prosecution and closure.

I had another burglary that was on a Friday and one of the things that had to be done was a photo lineup. A victim said he could possibly ID a suspect, so I put together a photo lineup and another officer working the next day volunteered to conduct the lineup. That's where teamwork comes in.

TCV: Is the typical backlog manageable?

Bocage: It is usually manageable. Zone integrity is a huge part of what we do. We may have three or four officers, rarely five in a zone at any one time. You need to make sure you get done what you need to get done and still be available to help in the zone. I have two cases I am working on now.

Mahboobi: I honestly don't know. I have a few that I want to follow up on that have been holding for a few weeks. With older cases, it may still be active, but you may not necessarily make all contacts. One of my cases has a witness who is now in Washington State. The police there are contacting that witness for me.

Snelson: Sometimes, due to a lack of investigative leads the case is suspended. The officer has the discretion to put the case in that disposition. A lot of times it will be discussed with other officers and sergeants to see if something has been overlooked. If you are able to dispose of a case then you will say if a crime did or did not occur. You will either forward the crime to the D.A. and ask for charging and file a complaint or close the case as 'unfounded' if proven that there was no crime.

Mahboobi: If you suspend a case and something comes about down the road, it may not come back to you. Another officer might get it and run with it using your report as a reference.

TCV: Is there a database of these files?

Snelson: Yes, a great example of this is a residential burglary that occurred a month before I got the call. A Contra Costa County Sheriff in Danville stopped a guy and found some of our victim's property on him and called an assist from our department. Some of the items had not been reported as lost. I was able to pull up the report from the original officer and then re-contacted the victim, wrote a supplemental report to the officer's suspended report that included additional items. It was all tied together in that way.

TCV: You have all successfully completed your FTO training and we will meet again in about six months after you have experienced a significant amount of time on your own in the field. Any further comments?

Bocage: I would like to thank my FTOs for a fantastic job, very encouraging, disciplined and tempered training. It has been a great experience for me. Starting from the top, I want to thank Officers Gregg Crandall, Miliano Marcelino, Tony Tassano, Roger Kellmann, Jill Wilkinson, Steve Solaro, Javier Marquez. I appreciate everything they have done for me and I want to thank everyone else in the department who helped me during this time. I am sure they will all be there for us in the future too. There are so many people in the department who have helped me; it is hard to name them all.

Mahboobi: As a whole, I can't say enough about the support of the department. This has to be the best training program, bar none. I don't know how they can improve this. Any more and it would drive you crazy and any less and you wouldn't have the confidence necessary to do the job. You have to go through a lot to become an FTO. These are veteran, experienced officers. There wasn't one FTO that as I sat in their car with them, I wasn't envious and impressed with their knowledge and ability to handle whatever comes their way. Every call I come away impressed with the fine qualities of the officers we have in our department.

I was fortunate to be trained by my primary FTO Officer Jim Koepf. Others included Officer Chris Hummel and the detectives I worked with, Detective [Fred] Bobbitt, [Frank] Noey, [Brian] Ancona, Sgt. [Dean] Cobet. In the Traffic Unit, I learned so much from Officer [Daniel] Harvey. In my third phase, I rode with Officer Gregg Pipp, Officer [Roger] Kellmann and Officer Dennis Alfonso (I want to con-gratulate Officer Alfonso who is retiring on December 29 after 29 plus years with the agency - he is a legend!). Sergeants [Jon] Lopes, [Chris] Mazzone, [William] Ernser; I also want to mention Captain Bob Nelson for his support. I would like to add

Sergeant [Kimberly] Petersen and in investigations, where I spent many, many hours, Detective [Mark] Dang as well as recovery with Detective [Donald] George and Officer [Paul] McCormick. The list goes on and on for all of us! I hope, someday, to stand beside these people and be half as good as they are at what we do.

Snelson: I echo everything that has been said by the others. This has been a well done and thought out program from the academic and intellectual side and the practical side. It is what I needed for the past six months. My list of FTO's; Officer [Norberto] Quimson was my primary. Also in my primary phase, I rode with Officers Glenn Miller and Caroline Montalbo. My secondary FTO was Officer [Kevin] Gott. My Traffic Officer was Officer Dennis Madsen; my tertiary was with Officer Joe Geibig and I also rode with Officer John Anderson. In Detective Division, I worked with Detective [James] Larkin and Detective [Mark] Dang and Detective [Jeremy] Miskella. I got a ton of information from every person I worked with. Every single officer had positive and encouraging things to say even when I screwed up. The comments were to learn from it to do a better job. It couldn't have been a better program or learning environment. A lot of it had to do with everyone, not just our FTOs. My sergeants were also very supportive; Sergeants [Robert] Lanci, [Patrick] Epps and [Antonio] Delgado.

Beyond Probation

A bit over six months ago, TCV completed a series of interviews with three "rookie" Fremont police officers who had just graduated from police academy training in Sacramento, CA. Matthew Bocage, Ramin Mahboobi and Matthew Snelson met with Tri-City Voice Publisher/Editor in Chief, William Marshak, every two weeks during their FTO (Field Training Officer) training to express their thoughts about the challenges of a particularly stressful period at the beginning of their career in law enforcement. The same group gathered on July 21, 2005 for a final meeting to reminisce, look forward to completion of their probation period and what lies beyond.

TCV: It has been six months since we last met. From your viewpoint, where are you now in relation to our last meeting?

Mahboobi: I am much more confident by far than when I was sitting in this chair seven months ago. However, every day is a learning experience. I am now able to tackle more complex projects and self-initiated activity. Seven months ago, I was feeling, 'Let's not dig up more trouble than I can handle. I need to focus on what I am dealt.' Now I am confident that I can handle the calls; it's all about learning to use the resources and information we have - how to obtain it and how to use it. We need to become familiar with the crooks out there; be aggressive to stop them and put them away.

Bocage: I agree one hundred percent. I would highlight two things

Ramin just mentioned. Getting to know the crooks is a sign that you have arrived. I look at the officers with the department and they really know the names, faces, who they are looking for and who those folks are associated with. During training, you are into a lot of things, but what you are, primarily, is a call taker. Being proactive is a challenge for me - a goal of mine - each and every day. Lieutenant [Gus] Arroyo gave an inspiring speech at a recent shift change. He said that we want criminals, criminal enterprise, to be uncomfortable operating and living in Fremont, period. We don't want it to be easy for them.

Snelson: I feel that I have the "child food" part down; I can handle basic calls. I know how to deal with certain situations. Now I am trying to get into the more complex things because that is what I think good police officers do. I am trying to be more proactive and stir things up; find the crime that is occurring beneath normal society. It is as the others said; trying to find crime and uncover it is a continual challenge. It is an exciting time.

TCV: For those who choose to apply for a position as a police officer, what qualities do you feel are necessary for success?

Snelson: You need the ability to listen and speak clearly to people; to interact. Common sense - to make logical decisions - is necessary as well as an understanding of what is going on and how to apply basic law. A good officer needs confidence, but not too much. A high drive, a desire to work and the ability to work with a team is essential. Even though you may ride alone, if too prideful to ask for help, you will never make a good police officer. The team aspect is huge.

Bocage: Perseverance is a big part of where we are right now. You need to work hard from the very beginning to the very end of every day. That has really paid off. If I was to speak to someone interested in this type of work I would emphasize this. Just don't quit. It really does pay off in the end.

Adaptability is another essential element. You have to be able to adapt in so many ways - work schedules, the variety of crimes and calls - you need to be able to adapt depending upon the personality of the person you are speaking with. You may go from one extreme to the other within a matter of minutes. People

going into this line of work should ask themselves if they have these two qualities intact.

Mahboobi: I echo what the others have said. You have to have a passion for the job. There is so much to challenge you in the beginning and throughout your career. If you are not truly dedicated to this career, you are not going to make it. That is where the difference lies. It is a complex job and requires so much from you. We are not superheroes to do this; we are just dedicated and didn't give up no matter what.

TCV: At this point in your career, do others around you treat you differently?

Mahboobi: My family is one hundred percent proud of me. I could not ask for any more support. They appreciate my hard work and have been there for me throughout my time at the academy and FTO program. My friends have all been great throughout my training.

It is only when you run into someone you haven't seen in a long time or are introduced to a new group of people - there is the awkward moment. For some reason, family and friends only know one way to introduce me; 'Hey, this is Ramin, he's a cop.'

I wish I could change that since it's an awkward introduction. That is the only negative thing I can think of with this career.

Bocage: I can relate to what Ramin just said. It is a really strange doorway you walk through. While police work is a lifestyle and you become accustomed to it, it is not as though I just hang out with cops. I hang out with a lot of other folks too. Police personnel are just good people doing a tough job; that is how I look at it.

I go through the same thing when meeting people. It is a great icebreaker and party conversation. Everybody wants to know 'have you shot anybody? How many dead bodies have you seen?' The typical things they have seen on television. They want you to share your experiences and, believe me, we have a lot of them - some are hilarious. They are a lot of fun to share. Police work is a brotherhood, but I don't feel as different as I used to. My family is very comfortable with it. They are very proud of me and love what I am doing. They understand the long hours and sacrifices that come with the job.

Snelson: It is a very polarizing job. Strong stereotypes can come into play when someone realizes you are a police officer. I have had both reactions - some people love you and you can tell that others have had bad experiences. It is tough when you are first introduced to people that way and they view you in a negative light right off the bat.

A case in point: my wife and I were just in Tahoe at a teppanyaki restaurant where they cook the food in front of you. We were the only ones at the table and the chef was talking with us and asked my wife about her profession. She replied that she is a teacher and he asked some normal questions about teaching. Then he turned to me and asked what I do. When I told him that I am a police officer, there was this pause and an awkward, "oh." You just don't know

what he is thinking; he was a young guy, about my age and he may be thinking that he didn't show up for traffic court and if I find out about that, I will arrest him.

Apart from the introduction side, there is a balance to be found. I try to turn it off; I don't need to be a cop around my family. I do, however, feel a little bit more aware and on guard, especially in Fremont. For example, my wife and I went out to dinner with another couple that we are friends with; his wife is eight months pregnant. We were sitting outside having dinner and a guy - a very violent person that I had arrested about three weeks earlier - walks by. I can guarantee that I am not on his "good" list. If he realizes who I am and decides to confront me, although I feel that I can handle myself, now I have to worry about my friend, my wife and his wife. There is some sensitivity there. On the other side, we just had an officer, Will Cannon, retire after 30 years service and to see the respect and honor from the rest of the officers is huge.

TCV: Any last thoughts before we close this interview and our series?

Snelson: I want to thank my wife and family for their support during this process; it is an enormous step to get through academy, FTO and now look toward the end of probation. It takes a lot of support to get through this and my wife has been awesome throughout. I couldn't ask for better partners to go through academy with me. The support of the department has been great. I feel that I have found the career I want to stay in for the next 28 1/2 years. I look forward to being involved in a lot of different things and keeping my mind active.

One of the midnight officers, John Anderson, said he loves the job because there is never a dull moment. There is always something going on that is making your mind work. The variables are always changing. It's exciting. I am constantly intellectually active and on the physical side as well. I have found the long term job for me.

Mahboobi: I look back from the beginning to where we are now and how we are only a fraction into this career. This experience, so far, has been amazing. There have been tremendous obstacles but looking back, I couldn't have asked for a better group to be with at the academy. We have formed a bond that will be there for the rest of our lives. Together, we conquered this. I don't know if I could have made it without their support, the support of my family and the department.

It is fun to look back, knowing my concerns and how difficult it was. Now I am proud to say I am here right now. This is definitely the career for me. I made the right decision and am still working hard to keep it. Every day brings new challenges.

Bocage: I agree with everything that has been said and would like to thank my family as well. It has been fantastic. I have had wonderful support from everyone, especially my future wife, Raquel Leon, throughout this entire process. I couldn't be happier than where I am. The camaraderie that I feel here

has made all the difference in the world to me.

I am very grateful to have shared the entire process with these two guys. They are my friends and a barometer of my career. The staff and department have been fantastic. I really feel that I have found a home here. My life has changed so much in such a short period of time. I am at the very beginning of a career and cannot wait to enjoy it. I couldn't be happier than I am right now. It feels really good to be sitting here with these two guys. I think we have quite a journey ahead of us and I can't wait to proceed down the path.

Editor's Note:

I would like to thank Officers Bocage, Mahboobi and Snelson for allowing me to enter their lives for a short while. It is my hope that this series of interviews can give our readers an appreciation for the rigors of preparation, training and the day-to-day activities of law enforcement personnel. I would also like to thank Sergeant Clarise Lew who facilitated the series and Chief Craig Steckler who lent his support and approval. Finally, I would like to thank all members of the Fremont Police Department and neighboring city police personnel in Newark and Union City for their support and encouragement.

Lt. Matt Snelson, Sgt. Matt Bocage, and Sgt. Ramin Mahboobi
August 2017

Final Thoughts

Reflecting over the past 14 years, if there is a common theme that has steadied our careers and maintained our enthusiasm for this profession, it is balance. Since we were first interviewed, we have gotten married and started families. The benefit and perspective that raising a family brings to the life of a law enforcement officer cannot be overstated. Resiliency is a difficult quality to cultivate, particularly if you attempt to do it by yourself. Endless hours of shift work and overtime can be grueling at times. Exposure to human tragedy and trending degradation of public trust in our authority can lead to cynical callousness if not properly balanced by the notion that we came to this department with; that we love this community and want to serve it by doing everything we can to keep it safe. Comfortingly, knowing that each of us has a loving and supporting family to go home to at the end of every day replenishes our commitment to stay the course.

The earlier days were exciting - high-speed pursuits, felony arrests, and high profile cases. Hard work led to specialized assignments, instructor positions, and promotion. The thrill of the chase has evolved into the satisfaction of crafting policy, of helping to develop future leaders, and of providing oversight in the safe execution of large-scale operations. Our goal for the remaining 10-12 years of our careers is simply to continue to work with our fellow officers to make our agency the best it can be. The citizens and community of Fremont deserve nothing less.

For those who may be reading this and considering a career in law enforcement we humbly offer this advice; keep an open mind, be principled and resolute, expect change, have empathy, be a perpetual student, and most importantly, lead a balanced life.

Respectfully

Matt, Ramin, & Matt

"Give justice to the weak and the fatherless; maintain the right of the afflicted and the destitute. Rescue the weak and the needy; deliver them from the hand of the wicked."

Psalm 82:3-4

"Whom shall I send? And who will go for us?"

And I said, "Here am I, send me."

Isaiah 6:8